The Greatest Gift Ever

CRAIG CANFIELD

Exulon ELITE

Copyright © 2016 by Craig Canfield

The Greatest Gift Ever

by Craig Canfield

Edited by Carolyn Abbott, WordsWork Consulting Group, Westminster MA.

Printed in the United States of America.

ISBN 9781498483032

All rights reserved solely by the author. The author guarantees all contents are original and do not infringe upon the legal rights of any other person or work. No part of this book may be reproduced in any form without the permission of the author. The views expressed in this book are not necessarily those of the publisher.

© All rights reserved. No part of this book may be reproduced in any form without permission in writing from the author, except in the case of brief quotations in critical articles or reviews.

www.xulonpress.com

Unless otherwise indicated, Scripture quotations taken from:

The NEW AMERICAN STANDARD BIBLE®, Copyright © 1960,1962,1963,1968,1971,1972,1973,1975,1977,1995 by The Lockman Foundation. Used by permission.

THE HOLY BIBLE, NEW INTERNATIONAL VERSION®, NIV® Copyright © 1973, 1978, 1984, 2011 by Biblica, Inc.® Used by permission. All rights reserved worldwide.

The New King James Version®. Copyright © 1982 by Thomas Nelson. Used by permission. All rights reserved.

The New Life Version Bible Copyright © 1969 by Christian Literature International. Used by permission.

The Holy Bible, New Living Translation, copyright © 1996, 2004, 2015 by Tyndale House Foundation used by permission.

The New Revised Standard Version Bible, copyright © 1989 the Division of Christian Education of the National Council of the Churches of Christ in the United States of America. Used by permission. All rights reserved.

The Voice™. Copyright © 2008 by Ecclesia Bible Society. Used by permission. All rights reserved.

ACKNOWLEDGEMENTS

A special thanks to everyone involved with this project, especially during the early stages. Loriann, your approval, support, and input during this entire endeavor meant the world to me. Kyle, your suggestions from the very first draft helped expand the material into what it ultimately became. Abby, I know this wasn't an easy read for you but your recommended changes helped to reach a different audience than I had originally envisioned. Cabot, as a mentor and friend, your input helped chisel away the rough edges from the material.

Numbers 6:24-26 – "The Lord bless you and keep you; the Lord make his face shine on you and be gracious to you; the Lord turn his face toward you and give you peace." (NIV)

Isaiah 40:31 – "…but those who wait for the Lord shall renew their strength, they shall mount up with wings like eagles, they shall run and not be weary, they shall walk and not faint." (NRSV)

Philippians 4:13 – "I can do all things because Christ gives me the strength." (NLV)

DEDICATION

This book is dedicated, first and foremost, to the one who was the inspiration behind it all, my Lord and Savior, Jesus Christ. I never would have had the ability to complete such an undertaking had this material not come from Him.

To my wife, Loriann, you are and always will be my better half. I don't know where I would be today had you not stayed by my side during all the ups and downs of our life together. You stuck it out when most people would have thrown in the towel and given up on me a long time ago. You truly are a great reflection of what it means to be a Christian and a wife. Your love, encouragement, commitment, and support over the years helped me finally become who God called me to be all along. You have my love and gratitude for eternity. I am, because you are.

To my daughters, Sarah and Robyn, I couldn't be prouder of the women you both have both turned out to be. Sarah, I wish you continued success with the amazing family you and your husband have started. Robyn, I hope that your future becomes all that you dreamed for and the one you've always wanted. Thank you both for your love and support over the years. I am the luckiest father ever.

Finally, to all the men and women serving our country in the US Armed Forces and to those in law enforcement, I pray that God keeps all of you safe each and every day. Thank you for your service and for protecting the very liberties all Americans enjoy. You are the first line of defense from those who seek to destroy the very foundation of our great nation.

Luke 1:37 – "For nothing will be impossible with God." (NRSV)

FOREWORD

The mere fact that I am writing this is totally a "God thing". When I think back to a few years ago, I would have never believed that my husband would become a man of God. Yes, Craig believed in God, but I saw no relationship there or real commitment to living a godly life.

The amazing changes I have seen in Craig as a result of his hard work the past few years bring me great joy. I am proud of the man of God he has become and of his passion for godly marriages, sharing the word of God with others and his love for his family.

I am excited for you to read this amazing story of this man's spiritual transformation. Craig and I hope that, through his story, you will discover how much you are loved by our heavenly Father, a love that requires nothing in return.

The Greatest Gift Ever

No matter where you are in your walk with God, this story will bring you to a new understanding of His love for all of us. There is no guarantee that life will be easy or that we will not face our share of trials and tribulations. Our prayers will not always be answered as quickly or have the outcomes we hoped for. I can guarantee that God will be by your side through the storms. By better understanding God's love for you, you will have the ability to trust in His timing and have peace during those difficult times that life throws at you. Believe me, one of the most difficult things I've dealt with during my walk of faith is patience. Craig will tell you, I am not a patient person, but I have learned to just be and let Christ do His amazing work. Craig's transformation into a godly man is one of those amazing works!

Now sit back, relax and enjoy what you are about to read. I promise that by the end of the book, if you follow the steps he lays out, you, too, will be transformed, full of hope and peace, knowing you are not alone in this crazy thing called life. We are all here to encourage one another to just be loved by our heavenly Father.

Blessings to all – Lori

Foreword

Job 27:6 – "I hold on to what is right and good and will not let it go. My heart does not put me to shame for any of my days." (NLV)

Luke 1:47 – "And my spirit is happy in God, the One Who saves from the punishment of sin." (NLV)

Romans 6:23 – "For the wages of sin is death, but the free gift of God is eternal life in Christ Jesus our Lord." (NRSV)

CONTENTS

Acknowledgements v
Dedication vii
Foreword ix
Introduction xv

The Story Behind the Story. 19
My Story 29
Our Story. 37
What I Thought I Knew 50
The Worldly View 54
The Greatest Gift Ever 61
Godly Love 68
    Love Is Patient 71
    Love Is Kind 76
    Love Does Not Envy 80
    Love Does Not Boast 85
    Love Is Not Proud. 88
    Love Does Not Dishonor Others 92
    Love Is Not Self-Seeking 96
    Love Is Not Easily Angered 100
    Love Keeps No Record of Wrong 104
    Love Does Not Delight in Evil. 112
    Love Rejoices in the Truth 116
    Love Always Protects. 120

The Greatest Gift Ever

    Love Always Trusts. 123
    Love Always Hopes 129
    Love Always Perseveres 136
    Love Never Fails 140
A New Perspective 143
    Achieving Godly Love 148
The Heart of the Matter. 151
My Journey 157
The Beginning of my Transformation 167
The Meeting 170
The Final Straw. 175
Our Renewal. 180
The End Result 184
Seeing Things Differently 186
Staying Focused 193
The Encounter That Changed Me Forever. 197
Why We Struggle 213
No More Excuses 218
Seeing Through God's Eyes. 228
Begin the Transformation 234
    Step One – loving God. 237
    Step Two – loving others 241
    Step Three – surrender all of you to God 243
    Step Four – leave your past behind 251
New Beginnings 254
    The Perfect Day 256
    A Perfect World. 259
I Choose Love. 265
My God 267
My Final Day. 270

Bibliography 273

INTRODUCTION

Next to once having to write an apology letter to my wife, Lori, this whole book endeavor was definitely one of the hardest things I've ever had to do: not because I didn't want to finish this once I began, but more because I never saw myself as someone who was qualified enough to ever write a book.

After all, who really wants to read something written by an ordinary Joe like me? What are my credentials? I'm not a theologian, scholar, doctor, or even a therapist. I'm just someone who, like most of us, has received more than their fair share of bumps, bruises, and hard knocks along that wonderful journey called life.

I never imagined I would have ever experienced a series of "from God" moments or even be privileged enough to witness a few burning bushes along the way. Whether you consider them to be good or bad experiences, I've had more than my fair share of them. Amazingly, all of these Godly experiences would eventually become the inspiration behind the writing of this book.

My hope for all who read this is that, in the end, the message will mean as much to you as it does to me. It has already helped change and shape me for the better. For once, I believe I am finally beginning to live my life as I should have been all along.

Regardless of how I got to where I am today, I find comfort knowing that I have always been a child of God after I was saved and baptized. Those credentials alone should be all I would ever need to write about my own journey, right? Hopefully, when we are finished, you will be the one who decides that for yourself.

John 1:12 – "Yet to all who did receive him, to those who believed in his name, he gave the right to become children of God — children born not of natural descent, nor of human decision or a husband's will, but born of God." (NIV)

Introduction

John 3:3 – "Jesus answered and said to him, 'Most assuredly, I say to you, unless one is born again, he cannot see the kingdom of God.' " (NKJV)

THE STORY BEHIND THE STORY

Since I've already indicated that this whole endeavor was a God thing and never a "me" thing, I need to share with you how all of this all came to be. God recently put me through a series of very unique situations. They all happened over a short period of time, one right after another. There was no rest in between each one, and each situation seemed to be harder to overcome than the last one. Little did I know it at the time, but God was going to rock my world through all of them, and my life would finally be changed forever as a result.

My first unique situation started when our church pastor sent me a letter asking me to participate in an upcoming, church-sponsored leadership development course. At first I thought surely he had the

The Greatest Gift Ever

wrong person. Maybe his letter was really intended for Lori. I never considered myself as someone who would to be viewed as a potential future leader within our church. Sure, I led a few Bible studies here and there but, for the most part, I usually just quietly went to church without being involved with any other pomp and circumstance. After the initial shock wore off, I realized that the pastor had, in fact, sent the letter to me. If that wasn't enough cause for alarm after I finished reading his invitation letter, I learned that this whole journey was going to require a year-long commitment from me.

As the many excuses started to run through my head as to why I couldn't possibly commit to participating in the course, I became even more alarmed after learning that I would be required to read several books. Along with the required readings, there would also be mandatory monthly meetings to discuss and debate each book. The whole situation seemed too daunting to me, and my first reaction was that I would have to come up with some dignified excuse as to why I couldn't possibly fulfill his request.

The main reason for my initial inclination to decline participating in the course centered on all that required reading. Don't get me wrong, there is nothing unusual about those of you out there who like to read; however, I am not one of them. It is very hard for me to concentrate long enough to finish reading anything beyond a newspaper or magazine article and, yes, pictures make all the difference in the world for me. Up until that point in my life, I could probably count on both hands the number of books I had ever read cover to cover.

Needless to say, I had myself thoroughly convinced that this course wasn't going to be for me. It would be too stressful, and the task at hand seemed too impossible for me to complete. I certainly didn't want to set myself up for failure by taking on more than I could handle. But after discussing the course with Lori and also praying about the whole situation, I surprisingly felt led to give it all a go and told the pastor he could count me in.

Trying to get a jump on the reading, I ordered all the books in advance. Once they arrived, I stacked them in order according to how they were going to be read. Some books were bigger and thicker than the others. Based upon their titles, some books looked like they would easier to read compared to some of the others.

At first sight, the pile was pretty high, and the doubter inside me again tried to convince my hopeful side that I could never possibly read all these books. When would I find the time to read all of them? What would I do if I couldn't finish reading a book because it failed to captivate me? Or, heaven forbid, what if the book turned out to be too complicated for me to comprehend? How was I going to avoid becoming a procrastinator and ultimately fall behind by failing to complete the required readings on time? My list of questions and doubts grew as the time drew nearer for the course to start. Little did I know at the time, but God was going to work out my reading plan for me. The scary part was I didn't even have to ask.

My second unique situation arose shortly after I committed to participating in the leadership course. During my time working as a police officer, I had suffered several knee injuries through those years which usually required arthroscopic knee surgeries. Those injuries and surgeries eventually forced me to leave a job I truly enjoyed but was unable to continue doing physically. Thankfully, God saw fit to put me into another job working for a Fortune 100 company where the physical demands on my body were much less strenuous.

The Story Behind the Story

Despite this, my knee was not improving, so God orchestrated my decision to finally undergo a long overdue knee replacement. Those of you who have been through this procedure or have had a similar situation can probably empathize with the whole ordeal. I had put off having the surgery for many years, because my doctor felt I was too young and he didn't want me to have to undergo another replacement later in life. We tried several intervention strategies to postpone the surgery for as long as possible. Some of those interventions provided temporary relief from the pain, while some of them didn't work at all. The constant pain and discomfort eventually wore me down, and God's plan for my knee ultimately won in the end. I met with my doctor and scheduled a date for my long overdue knee replacement.

As luck would have it, I only needed a partial replacement, but I didn't know that outcome for certain until after the surgery was completed. After the surgery, I began my agonizing road to recovery with intense physical therapy sessions several days a week. Things initially went very well, and I planned on returning to work in about a month. Unfortunately, I experienced several setbacks during this time, and my recovery took a lot longer than I had originally expected.

Without my realizing it at the time, God was quietly at work behind the scene. Not only was He giving me the extra time I needed to fully recover from the surgery, but He was also taking care of the time I needed to give my full attention to those reading requirements for the leadership course. The additional time away from work didn't just allow me to finish reading the first book in the course; surprisingly, it also allowed me to finished reading all of them in about three months. To this day, I am still amazed at how God orchestrated my whole reading plan. He gave me not only the time to read each book but also the desire to finish reading each and every book from cover to cover.

Most of the books were easy to read. Only a few were a little more difficult to read because the subject matter was very foreign to me. Still, all in all, each book served a unique purpose as part of the whole leadership course and, when it was all said and done, I was glad I had read each one of them. I learned so much from all these books. In fact I'd have to say that the leadership course, the books, the monthly meetings, and the extra time away

The Story Behind the Story

from work recovering from the surgery all significantly contributed to my growing as a Christian like I'd never grown before. The best part of it all for me was that none of this growth would have been possible without God being in control of it from the start.

Finally, the last unique situation that arose out of God's plan for me was probably one of the most difficult work situations I have ever experienced. After finally being released by my doctor to return to work, I did so only to discover that my position within the company was being eliminated. This certainly wasn't the type of New Year I had envisioned or something I ever imagined having to deal with. To say I was in shock when I first got the news would be an understatement. It was extremely difficult having to inform Lori that I no longer had a job. Thankfully, the company let me go with a nice severance package that would allow me to provide for my family for several months. I found myself unemployed for the first time in my life, and I had no idea what my next steps were or how I was going to provide for my family. I was very angry that the company could treat an employee that way, so the whole situation never felt right to me.

As you can imagine, I didn't exactly deal with that experience the best way I could have. There were days I was glad to have the extra time with my family, and then there were days when my anger got the best of me. After allowing me to feel sorry for myself for a little while, God didn't cut me any more slack. Not only did He continue to provide for all of my family's needs in ways I would never have imagined after losing my job, but He also continued to complete the work He began in me at the very beginning of this whole journey.

Some of the most amazing things began happening to me. After going through several unique and difficult situations one right after another in a very short amount of time, I began to change. The best part of it all was that Lori and the girls noticed the change in me as well. My faith didn't just grow; it took off like a rocket. I began to grow inside by leaps and bounds. I was on fire for God like never before. I wanted the whole world to know it and, for the first time in my life, I wasn't too shy to share it all with others.

Don't get me wrong. I've experienced growth throughout my Christian journey before but never anything quite like this. I finally had all the time in

The Story Behind the Story

the world I could have ever hoped for to spend with God and continue to grow in my relationship with Him. Without all of these unique situations happening one after the other, I doubt I would have grown as I had or as quickly as I did. I also don't feel I would be as close to God as I am today. It was because of this recent growth and my subsequent transformation that God became the inspiration behind the writing of this book.

Not only did He inspire the writing of this book, but He also instilled in me the desire to take all of this new growth to the next level. After many prayers and discussions with Lori, we decided to take our marriage experience to the next level by becoming marriage advocates within our church. Along with three other couples, we formed a Life Group/Bible Study within our church called Marriage Warriors. Our belief is that we can help other Christian married couples as a group. Our goal is to assist all the marriages that are thriving by keeping them thriving and to assist all the marriages that are struggling so they too can begin to thrive again. We believe that God will lay the foundation for our group, and He will take our whole endeavor to where He wants it to go. Even though our group is still in its infancy, our future looks very promising. We can't wait to see what God has in store for

Marriage Warriors and how we will positively impact all the marriages within our church.

Psalm 51:7, 10-12 – "Cleanse me with hyssop, and I will be clean; wash me, and I will be whiter than snow. Create in me a pure heart, O God, and renew a steadfast spirit within me. Do not cast me from your presence or take your Holy Spirit from me. Restore to me the joy of your salvation and grant me a willing spirit, to sustain me." (NIV)

Ecclesiastes 11:5 – "Just as you do not know the path of the wind or how the bones are made of a child yet to be born, so you do not know the work of God Who makes all things." (NLV)

Jeremiah 29:11-13 – "For I know the thoughts that I think toward you, says the LORD, thoughts of peace and not of evil, to give you a future and a hope. Then you will call upon Me and go and pray to Me, and I will listen to you. And you will seek Me and find *Me*, when you search for Me with all your heart." (NKJV)

1 Peter 5:7 – "Since God cares for you, let Him carry all your burdens and worries." (VOICE)

MY STORY

As I indicated earlier, I am so fortunate and grateful that I have been a child of God since my early teenage years. When I was 12 years old, my family was living in the small town of Hawthorne, Nevada. It might sound just a little bit foolish, but I only initially started going to a local church in town because a girl I was interested in went there. Our relationship didn't last very long, yet I kept attending that church. Something drew me there each Sunday. After a few months, I finally turned my life over and accepted Jesus Christ as my Lord and Savior.

I wish I could say that my early Christian journey was just as amazing as it is today, but that would be stretching the truth a lot, to say the least. The church I attended didn't provide any Christian guidance or direction after I became saved. Their philosophy was for me to go out and save others, but they didn't provide any guidance or direction about how to accomplish that mission. They believed that the Holy Spirit would guide my path and that anything else I needed would be provided by God. I tried walking by faith as best as I could without the advantage of having an arsenal of "Godly" tools to utilize in my Christian tool belt. Needless to say, I wasn't very successful trying to move forward on my own.

I never learned what was in the Bible except what I heard being preached at church. What I did learn about the Bible from those sermons usually dealt with readings from the Old Testament. I tried a few times to read the Bible on my own, and we already know how much I enjoy reading. Like most novices, I started reading the Bible from the beginning. My enthusiasm quickly faded after a few chapters, and my Bible soon became very dusty as it sat in its place on my bookshelf.

Without continued growth, my faith never expanded beyond what I already believed when I was saved. I soon stopped going to church and tried living out my teenage years on my own instead of allowing God to lead the way. In time, I lost that intimate connection I once had with God. Since I never

My Story

learned who God was and who I was in Christ, my perception of God changed and I also changed. That, more than anything, had a very profound impact on my early Christian journey.

My concept and understanding of who God was became flawed. When I fell back into living my life in sin, like most of us I felt ashamed and embarrassed, because deep down inside I knew what I was doing was wrong. As I continued to struggle, I soon felt undeserving of my salvation. My life soon resembled a ship in a storm without a rudder, and my course changed as each wave slammed against my bow. Instead of allowing God to take command and steer me clear to safety, I continually fought Him as I tried in vain to convince myself that I was the one who was in control and not Him.

My belief in who God really was soon seemed only to invoke images of an angry God. The God I had learned about always seemed to be struggling to love His people because they continually angered and disappointed Him. No matter what miracles God performed or what laws He put in place for them to live by, time and time again His people failed to change their ways to live in harmony with God. My life began to resemble the Israelites. Time and time again I failed to live in harmony with God, because I hadn't changed my ways.

As my journey continued, I began to view God as if He were the same as my earthly father. My father and I had a relationship that was far from perfect. I know now that he loved me as best he knew how because of the way he was raised. His father was apparently even less loving than mine. The things I remember most wanting and needing to hear from him was that he loved me and was proud of me. When I would accomplish something special and I didn't hear those words from him, it only made me try harder to please him over and over again. Just as in my relationship with God, I wanted to please Him all the time. I wanted to feel that He loved me and was proud of me. When I didn't feel that way because of my sin or because I wasn't growing, it made me feel farther away from God instead of closer to Him.

As a result, my Christian foundation was flawed, and my subsequent life became very shaky. I had assumed that I would immediately become a "perfect" person after I was saved, and that I wouldn't want to live anymore in the world like I used to. My life going forward would be side by side with God, and each day would be better than the last. Talk about setting myself up for failure, right? No matter how much I tried, my days were less than perfect. I couldn't stop feeling like a failure. The more I stumbled, the farther away from God I felt. The farther away from God I felt, the less I felt like trying. It was a never-ending battle, and the longer it went on, the more discouraged and frustrated I became.

If all that wasn't enough, I also never learned about the true purpose and the meaning behind prayer. I thought you prayed to God for anything and everything. So my prayers became a direct reflection of my lack of growth and understanding. I prayed that my favorite sports team would win a game or that a certain young lady would go out with me. I didn't know that although we can pray to God for anything, I should have been praying for continued Christian growth, wisdom, and development instead of just selfish worldly prayers.

To make matters even worse, I had very few Christian friends to learn from. Those people that I mainly associated with were definitely walking in the world and not with God. I also didn't have any family to teach me how to make my Christian journey better. Although my parents said that they

The Greatest Gift Ever

attended church growing up, we didn't. I knew my dad was a Methodist and my mom's background was Lutheran, but that was about as far as it went. I never knew where they stood in their faith, because it wasn't ever shared.

Without the necessary knowledge to fuel the fire I had when I was saved, my walk soon resembled a small smoldering fire compared to the huge roaring one it was in the beginning. Soon I found myself walking in the world more than I was walking in union with God. I allowed Satan to constantly defeat me by listening to his lies and believing I wasn't worthy of my salvation. Through it all, luckily my faith was never too far from my heart. Thankfully, with God's intervention I was able to sustain my faith just enough to help me get through the majority of those ups and downs during my younger years.

Despite the challenges I faced in my early Christian journey, I was very fortunate to have grown up as a military officer's brat, thanks to my father's 22-year US Air Force career. I was born at what used to be Kincheloe Air Force Base in Michigan's Upper Peninsula. Today my birthplace no longer exists, as the base was deactivated a number of years ago. During my father's career, we were privileged to move from base to base every few years. I enjoyed most of the places our family was stationed, while others were just okay. One of my favorite places was Ramstein Air Force Base in Germany. Being stationed there gave our family the opportunity to visit some nearby countries as well as to travel about Germany and experience its people and culture. The best part about living in a lot of different places growing up was not only the many places we got to see but also the opportunity to meet so many new people at each duty station.

In 1983, my father was assigned back to Michigan. I stayed there until I graduated from high school in 1985. Afterwards I tried the college routine by attending a university in New Mexico for a year. Unfortunately, being so far away from home by myself for the first time really took its toll on me. In the spring of 1986, I decided to relocate with my family who were now living in central Pennsylvania. I attended a local community college in the area for one semester, but I was never too serious about it. At 18, I certainly had no idea what I wanted to study, let alone what I wanted to do with the rest of my life.

Matthew 6:33 – "But seek first the kingdom of God and His righteousness, and all these things shall be added to you." (NKJV)

Philippians 4:6-7 – "Do not be anxious about anything, but in every situation, by prayer and petition, with thanksgiving, present your requests to God. And the peace of God, which transcends all understanding, will guard your hearts and your minds in Christ Jesus." (NIV)

Hebrews 11:1-3 – "Now faith is being sure we will get what we hope for. It is being sure of what we cannot see. God was pleased with the men who had faith who lived long ago. Through faith we understand that the world was made by the Word of God. Things we see were made from what could not be seen." (NLV)

OUR STORY

After moving back in with my family in Pennsylvania, I soon settled back into the swing of things. After a brief vacation, I knew I needed to find a job. I started working at a local McDonalds. Ironically, that McDonalds would become the launching point for our story, as this is where Lori and I first met. Initially, we were only coworkers but, thankfully, that didn't last long.

Sometime in late July, I was at that very McDonalds getting something to eat, and I happened to be in line at Lori's register. Little did I know at the time, but something was going to unfold between us that even I wasn't expecting. To make matters even more interesting, I was there along with a young lady I had been dating for a little when this whole unforeseen event began to play itself out.

Before Lori took my order, I looked up at her and for some reason she struck me as very different that day. She looked so beautiful. Her face seemed to glow and her blue eyes were sparkling more than ever. I was awestruck. Her smile instantly melted my heart. When she took my order, I was mesmerized with her words. I thought to myself that I had to ask her out, somehow, some way. All of this raced through my mind and, as odd as that was, the fact that I was in line with another woman never even entered into the picture.

I still couldn't get Lori out of my mind after leaving McDonalds. I can jokingly say today that Cupid's arrow definitely pierced my heart and that the angels above were singing "ah" in unison, but something unexplainable definitely happened. Whatever unfolded, without a doubt it was definitely one of those "ah ha" moments that you never forget.

As reality soon set in, I thought to myself that Lori would never go out with me. After all, she had an unblemished reputation. She was popular and very well known. When we first met a few months prior, I knew she was engaged to a guy she'd been dating since high school. I didn't know her availability at the time, which didn't really matter to me much. As we got to know each other a little better by working together, I always thought she was pretty and very nice but definitely someone who was out of my league. I kept thinking that, although I'm not the worst person in the world, Lori would not be interested in someone like me because I was the new kid in town, and we seemed so very different from each other.

From there I started convincing myself that Lori was exactly the type of woman I needed in my life. She was perfect in every way. Lori would help me put my "bad boy" tendencies aside and walk a straight line. I was convinced that dating Lori would somehow make me a better person all around.

After making some inquiries about her availability with some of her friends, I learned that she was indeed single and available. Jackpot baby! I eventually got her telephone number from one of her friends. After a few days, I finally summoned up the courage and called her. I was a nervous wreck as I dialed her number. I kept praying that no one would answer and I'd be able to leave a message instead. Thankfully, she did pick up the phone and, after a brief time of awkwardness, even I couldn't have envisioned how things would eventually turn out.

We talked as if we'd known each other for years. The whole conversation didn't last too long, but it sure felt like it. There seemed to be a connection between us from the start, although I still think her friends tipped her off to expect a call from me so she may have been a lot better prepared than I was. I finally got around to asking her out on a date and, to my surprise, she agreed to go out with me. Crazy I know, but it's true. As they say, the rest is history.

Saturday night, August 9, 1986, was our first date. We went to a late movie and then midnight bowling. I don't remember what movie we saw. I was a nervous wreck inside, but I didn't want her to know that. The whole night was simply amazing. We seemed to connect even more, and talking was definitely not a problem for either of us. I don't remember a moment that entire night where we weren't talking about anything and everything. We had such a great date, and the night seemed to fly by. My only issue the entire time came after we were finished at the bowling alley. Can you believe that she had the nerve to beat me at bowling? I still believe I let her win to make the night go better, so at the time it didn't matter to me much. But every now and then she likes to rub it in and remind me about it. The nerve, huh?

I don't remember where the time went, but before we knew it, we were back in the McDonalds parking lot talking until the very early morning hours. To make matters worse, we both had to work that same morning on what would turn out to be very little sleep. Thankfully, the thought of little sleep didn't seem to bother either one of us.

I don't think I slept at all before work. I was on Cloud 9 and rising. I had never met someone so interesting and amazing. She was perfect in every way. Beautiful, intelligent, confident, and as if that weren't enough, she also turned out to be a Christian too. Oh, and did I mention that she was also the Homecoming Queen at her high school her senior year? Man, I had hit the jackpot. I thought to myself, here is a person who I felt I could settle down with, and all of that after only our first date!

On Saturday, September 6, 1986, we went for a beach day trip to Ocean City, Maryland. It was an awesome trip and a perfect day. The weather turned out to be beautiful all day, and our time at the beach was just as nice. We stopped at a Burger King on the way home to grab a bite to eat. While we were there, something came over me, and suddenly I felt the urge to take our relationship to the next level.

Next thing I know I'm on one knee and proposing to her right there in the parking lot. To my relief, she said yes. I had no clue what came next, but I didn't care. We were only 18 at the time and hadn't been dating that long. There were so many unforeseen obstacles. I was sure I had found the love of my life, and now we were going to get married. Nothing else really mattered to me at that moment. We would figure out all the next steps together.

In January 1987, I enlisted in the US Navy and shortly afterwards shipped off to Great Lakes, Illinois, for boot camp. After completing boot camp, I was assigned to Yeoman Class "A" School in Meridian, Mississippi, in April 1987. It was very difficult for us to be apart, and our time away from each other felt like an eternity. Adding chaos to the mix was the fact that my next duty station after Yeoman training was still a big mystery, which made trying to plan a wedding anytime in our near future almost impossible. Needless to say that wasn't sitting too well with us, and we didn't want to put off our wedding anymore than we already had. So we got the brilliant idea that since we didn't want to wait to get married, we would elope instead.

Our Story

On April 25, 1987, we were married at the Courthouse in Jackson, Mississippi. Like our first date, I don't remember every detail because I was too nervous, so much so that I locked my keys in my car before the ceremony. Before we knew it, we were in front of a judge who performed our marriage ceremony. There wasn't anyone else present, just that judge and us. It turned out to be perfect in the end. There weren't any distractions or lots of people looking at us. It was just Lori and I looking into each other's eyes, reciting our vows to each other before God and that judge. We had no clue about what awaited us, but nothing really seemed to matter to us other than the fact that we were finally married.

Lori looked so beautiful in her dress, and I must say that I was dashing in my Navy summer white uniform. We were both only 19 years old at the time, so young and yet so in love. It had been just a little over eight months since we started dating, and almost half of that time I was away serving in the US Navy. Now we were married and without knowing it at the time, we were going to experience an interesting series of events. More on those interesting events later.

The Greatest Gift Ever

Being much wiser now compared to when we first started, we know we could have handled many of the hurdles we experienced in our early married years much better than we did. One of the biggest hurdles we eventually overcame was that, although Lori and I were both children of God, together we didn't firmly establish God at the head of our relationship and continue to grow together as a Christian couple. We didn't pray together, we didn't read the Bible together, and we never found a church to attend together. Our marriage soon mirrored the same experiences I faced in my younger Christian years. It was that same vicious cycle over and over again. The more I tried to live as a Christian while also still remaining in the world, the farther from God I felt. Needless to say our marriage back then was a far cry from what it has become today. Back then we survived from year to year, whereas today we both are growing spiritually at rates we could have only dreamed of when we were newly married.

Another hurdle soon became our families. Lori and I grew up very differently in many ways. My parents were still married when Lori and I began our life together. Unfortunately, her parents divorced while she was still in high school. Without realizing it then, that difference between us made each of us initially approach our marriage from different points of view. Lori believed that marriages didn't last, whereas I believed that all marriages lasted forever. It took some time but, thankfully, we both eventually landed on the same page and both learned to believe that our marriage would last until the end of our days.

We adopted that concept together, which has helped us get through many dark times. When others ask me the secret to being married for over 29 years, I jokingly tell them that Lori and I don't want the other one to win, so we stick it out. In reality, I believe not only our faith but also our not believing in divorce are huge factors in why we have lasted as long as we have, regardless of what we have gone through as a couple. I know that might not be the same for other couples, and that is fine. Not every marriage is the same, and we respect that. For us, it has been a blessing to know that no matter what we have experienced as a couple, we were always in this to win it, so to speak.

Surprisingly, we never saw our families as becoming hurdles in our marriage when we first began, but they were. Lori's family on her mother's side often had many family get-togethers in any given year, so she was used to that growing up. I grew up rarely seeing much of my mother's or father's family. When we were assigned to our first duty station in Norfolk, Virginia, this was Lori's first time away from her mother and father. Her mother wanted her to come home a lot more than what I felt we needed to for those family get-togethers. Needless to say, our differences on that issue unfortunately became the source of a few heated arguments. Lori was stuck in the middle of trying to balance my needs with her mother's needs. That put a lot of unnecessary pressure on Lori, and it became a hurdle for us that wasn't resolved for quite some time.

An additional difference between our families was that I remember hearing my parents verbally fight one time in their 26 years of marriage. Lori, on the other hand, had grown accustomed to seeing and hearing her parents fight often during theirs. Her parents weren't very affectionate towards one another in the presence of others. I wouldn't say my parents were overly affectionate in front of us, but I do remember them often kissing, holding hands, embracing, or lying together on the couch while watching television.

Another unforeseen hurdle occurred as a result of us returning back home often for those family get-togethers. We unfortunately allowed our families to have way too much influence on us. Instead of us learning to rely on each other to get through our first few marriage hurdles, we also included our families in those hurdles. Needless to say, with so many people involved in our business there also came many different attitudes, opinions, and recommendations. To say that resulted in a little conflict between Lori and me would certainly be an understatement. Still, in time we also learned to overcome that hurdle.

Today we realize that all marriages aren't perfect, and ours certainly isn't, either. We have had to weather our fair share of storms along the way. There have been many moments in my marriage when I wasn't at my best or acting the way I should have. I am ashamed to admit today that there were often times when I was selfish and put my needs in front of my family's. But what has remained perfect in our marriage is the love that we both have inside for each other. It has been the glue that has bonded us together from the very beginning. Thankfully, our love for each other saw us through it all, regardless of those many obstacles or hurdles that lined our path.

Looking back on it all now, Lori and I both agree that we would still do it all over again. Although we can admit today that we were certainly naïve about many things, we are thankful that we always held firm to our belief that our faith and our love for each other could see us through anything. As tough as some of our early marriage experiences were, everything changed for the better as soon as God was placed at the head of our marriage. That doesn't mean that we still don't experience difficult times in our marriage today. The difference for us today is how we better handle those difficulties.

Okay, so now you're wondering about the title of this book and what the greatest gift ever is, right? You're correct if you guessed Lori. Way to go. Unfortunately, as much as I want to say she is the greatest gift I have ever received, that statement is only partially true. So then, what do I consider that to be? I believe that the ***greatest gift ever*** is ***God's love*** for each and every one of us.

Jeremiah 33:3 – "Call to me and I will answer you, and will tell you great and hidden things that you have not known." (NRSV)

John 15:9 – "As the Father has loved me, so I have loved you; abide in my love." (NRSV)

1 Corinthians 16:14 – "Let all you do be done in love." (NASB)

WHAT I THOUGHT I KNEW

Probably the most frustrating thing I can admit today is that I never really had a clue what love was when I was younger. I thought I did, especially as love pertained to marriage. I only remember my parents arguing that one time, so I assumed that once they were married, couples rarely fought, if ever. If couples were fighting, then it must mean that they really don't love one another. For me, love in a marriage simply meant that you got along with your spouse and took care of their needs.

That concept was always reinforced in the things I saw growing up. I never witnessed any of my extended family or my friend's parents fighting. I grew up watching television shows like Happy Days, The Brady Bunch, The Love Boat, or The Carol Burnett Show. I don't ever remember seeing married couples in those shows fighting. I was raised in a military family, and I never witnessed any other married military couples fighting. Maybe some of you might feel I grew up a little bit sheltered, but seeing married couples fighting wasn't something I was ever exposed to. I held onto that fairy tale notion that all married couples got along. I believed for the longest time that all marriages were happy-go-lucky relationships each and every day. Without a doubt, my beliefs definitely influenced all my dating relationships prior to Lori. If my girlfriend and I fought, then it must have meant that we weren't truly "in love." That was the clue that it was time to move on to the next relationship. Looking back on it now, I must admit that I was a little naïve when it came to love and relationships. But during my younger years, I thought I knew it all. Didn't you?

Don't we all believe that we are love experts, no matter how old we are at the time? After all, how hard can love really be? Love is easy. It's one of mankind's oldest and most basic of all of our feelings. You meet someone, develop feelings for them, you sweep them off their feet, and visa versa. Bam, you're in love and all the rest is easy p'easy, right?

Somewhere along the way, you convince yourself that you can't live without the one you love. You can't get them off your mind. You always want to be with them. You can't wait to talk to them or, in today's world, have endless hours of "text" discussions. Soon you discover that you seem to have so much in common. They like, or pretend to like without you knowing at the time, all the same things you do. If they have any flaws, you certainly don't see any, because you're too busy chasing them to notice. You soon discover how your heart seems to race as you're driving to see them. Oh, and when you're finally together again, forget about it. I'm sure many of us can relate to that. After all, isn't that "amore"? Oh, how we sadly discover as we age that things we thought we knew, we actually had no clue about in the end.

I can't speak for your life experiences regarding love, but I know I had that exact concept of love, probably up until the very first time Lori and I had our first disagreement after we were married. I wish I could say that I remember what we argued about. In the end it doesn't matter. The shocking reality for me at the time was that I felt like a failure, because fighting with my spouse was such a foreign concept to me. I know a huge part of me was concerned that there was something wrong with me. All I knew was that I had to "fix it." In my eyes, couples in love, especially married couples, just didn't fight.

My love expertise growing up may have been very different from yours. Hopefully, there are a few out there who can relate to my understanding of love during my younger years. Regardless of where you find yourself, why should your understanding or your experiences with love ever be anything other than what it was meant to be, no matter how old you are at the time? To understand love better, we need to view how the world sees love.

Isaiah 55:8-9 – "For my thoughts are not your thoughts, neither are your ways my ways, saith Jehovah. For as the heavens are higher than the earth, so are my ways higher than your ways, and my thoughts than your thoughts." (ASV)

John 1:17 – "For the law was given through Moses, but God's unfailing love and faithfulness came through Jesus Christ." (NLT)

THE WORLDLY VIEW

~~~~~~

How we all view love as it pertains to marriage seems to change over time, just as it initially did for me. Not too long ago, lifetime marriages seemed to be the norm in our society. Today, they seem to be so rare that others feel as though a couple who has been married over twenty years deserves a Pulitzer Prize or some other type of honor. Today, encountering someone who is divorced or in a subsequent marriage feels like the norm, compared to someone who has been married for many years. I believe that one significant factor for this so-called tipping of the scales involves how couples choose to apply love to their marriages.

Would you be surprised to know that our society's use and definition of love is very different from how it is used in other places? We seem to use the word love so much and attach it to so many different situations and/or things. Some might say that we over use it, and I tend to agree. Now, let's look at some simple love definitions:

- a feeling of strong or constant affection for a person
- attraction that includes sexual desire
- the strong affection felt by people who have a romantic relationship
- a person you love in a romantic way
 (*merriam-webster.com*)

However you slice it, our concept of love merely boils down to having a deep affection or a deep attachment to someone or something. I can't speak for everyone, but today's worldly view of the meaning of love and how it ultimately affects all of the relationships we experience in our lifetime had me totally confused for the longest time. Why? Like most of us, I just didn't get it. Today our society seems to add more and more meanings and throws the word love around as if it was merely a passing fad. Usually when I hear someone speak about loving something, it begins to sound more like they have a strong "like," instead of there being that deep affection or that deep attachment.

Did you ever really sit down and think about love and what it seems to mean to so many people today? We are bombarded daily with someone's concept of what love is. You can listen to a variety of songs from many different genres that will describe love in so many different ways, or you can watch a variety of so-called "chick flicks" that also seem to provide a variety of perspectives about love. If that's not enough, you can surf the Internet or read a book for even more different perspectives on love. Our search of references on love could feel like it would take an eternity to dissect them all, which could certainly end up being the case.

If you want to have some fun with this whole love concept, just ask a child what love means, then add some spice to your curiosity by asking some teenagers what love means to them. But, you certainly can't stop there — you have to take it all one final step by asking some adults what they believe love means. If you want a whole new perspective on what love may mean to another, I'm positive you will discover many new definitions to enhance your own understanding of love by asking someone who

The Worldly View

just ended their relationship with a loved one. I don't doubt that you'll be as surprised as I was to hear the many different ways people try to describe what love means to them.

With that all being said, we can finally return to what lies at the heart of the message contained within this book. What would you now say is the greatest gift ever? Some might say Lori or our marriage, and as much as I would like to say yes, unfortunately, she's only part of the whole equation. If you said love was the core message, then you're definitely on the right track. But if you went just a little bit further and also gave credit to God for creating love, then, my friend, you've earned a gold star. If you thought anything else, then you need to start at the beginning of this book and read it all again. (Just kidding!) The correct answer, then, becomes that ***God's love*** for each and every one of us ***is*** without a doubt ***the greatest gift ever***.

Not only is God's love the greatest gift ever, but I truly believe that if we all learned to love as God loves, that would also force us to consider some follow-up questions. My favorite one is, how different would our lives here on earth be if we all learned to love as God loves? Would each of us become a better Christian? How much more harmonious would our time be here on earth if we, too, learned to love as God loves?

I didn't want to stop there, so I expanded my search about my new understanding of the greatest gift ever. I was surprised to learn how differently love was viewed in some other societies compared to ours. For example, ancient Greece used five different words to describe the various types of love within their society.

The first is *agape,* which means brotherly love, charity; the love of God for man and of man for God. In Christianity, agape would be used to describe God's unconditional love for His children. Another Greek word for love is *eros,* which describes having a sexual passion for someone. Interesting as well is that the modern Greek word *erotas*, from which the word erotic is derived, means intimate love. *Philia* is another Greek word used to describe love; it involves having an affectionate regard for or friendship with someone. Finally, the Greek word *storge* refers to the love and affection between parents and their children (*wikipedia.org)*.

There are also many different words used within the Hebrew language to describe love. I will focus our

The Worldly View

attention on the one Hebrew word that best supports my belief that the greatest gift ever is God's love for each one of us. That Hebrew word for love is *ahava,* and it has a very special meaning. Depending upon which resource you view, ahava consists of more than one word which, when combined, together form one word. Ahava essentially means both I give and I love. The ultimate meaning behind the Hebrew word ahava is that love is giving. Not only is love giving, but the actual process of giving helps the relationship develop into a much greater connection between the giver and the receiver.

Ahava should also be viewed from two different concepts. The first involves ahava from God. This literally transforms into the understanding that God gives His love to us. The second concept is the ahava we have towards another. The best example of what this type of ahava would look like to us involves the giving of love from a husband to his wife and visa versa. Each one gives their love to the other. The more the couple gives love to one another, the greater the ahava becomes between them.

Romans 8:38-39 – "For I am convinced that neither death, nor life, nor angels, nor principalities, nor things present, nor things to come, nor powers, nor height, nor depth, nor any other created thing, will be able to separate us from the love of God, which is in Christ Jesus our Lord." (NASB)

THE GREATEST GIFT EVER

So then, what is Godly love and how would Godly love appear to us? We already learned that God's love for each one of us is unconditional and consists of giving. Here is why I consider His love to be the greatest gift ever. God's is always unconditionally giving love to us *no matter what*. The greatest example of God's love lies at the core of our Christian beliefs:

John 3:16 – "For God so loved the world that he gave his one and only Son, that whoever believes in him shall not perish but have eternal life." (NIV)

I don't know about you, but to me, this deserves our best and loudest Amen! For me, there is no

The Greatest Gift Ever

better example of what God's unconditional giving love would look like to us.

I know there are many out there who would argue that the gift of our salvation would qualify as the greatest gift ever, and part of me would agree with you. However, take a step outside the box and analyze the first part of that verse, "for God so loved the world." If we break it down to its very essence, I believe it proves beyond any doubt that God's love came before the next greatest gift, which would then definitely be our salvation.

Another way to view it is to ask yourself the following question: would we have our salvation through the sacrifice of our Lord Jesus Christ if God didn't first so unconditionally give love to all of us before allowing His son to become the final, ultimate sacrifice to atone for our sins? This greatest gift of God's unconditional love finally allowed all of us, both Jews and gentiles, to become one with God forever. God loved us so much that He was willing to make that sacrifice so that, once and for all, we would have the opportunity to become His children. He did this because He always loves all of His children unconditionally, no matter what.

The Greatest Gift Ever

Unlike human love, God's love also comes without any additional strings attached. He does not attach His emotions or feelings to it, either. There are no "what if's," "buts," or "He does because we did" clauses. Thankfully, there are no prenuptials attached, either.

Even more amazing is that God's love is free. It ultimately boils down to our choice. God allows each of us to choose to join His family during any moment of our lives. The best part of God's love for me that I treasure the most is that, no matter what I do, His love for me remains steadfast despite the fact that I know I do not deserve it. Why don't I deserve it? Because I am human and, as such, at my very core I am nothing more than a saint who sins. But as a child of God, I know that my sins are forgiven. Doesn't that deserve another Amen?!

How amazingly Godlike each of us would become if we, too, could learn to love the way our God already loves all of us. Can you picture how different our world today would be if we all could achieve that goal? The possibilities for a more perfect world would be endless.

1 John 4:7-12 – "Dear friends, let us love one another, for love comes from God. Everyone who loves has been born of God and knows God. Whoever does not love does not know God, because God is love. This is how God showed his love among us: He sent his one and only Son into the world that we might live through him. This is love: not that we loved God, but that he loved us and sent his Son as an atoning sacrifice for our sins. Dear friends, since God so loved us, we also ought to love one another. No one has ever seen God; but if we love one another, God lives in us and his love is made complete in us." (NIV)

So our journey together now boils down to accepting the simple fact that the greatest gift ever is God's unconditional love for each and every one of us. The key to understanding that statement is twofold. First, God is love. Second, love comes from God. Each part combined reveals that the greatest gift ever is God's unconditional giving of His love to each one of us, no matter what.

I can't say it any better than that. The bottom line is, God is love and love comes from God. Can I get another Amen?! If you say you love, then God has to also be inside of you. The only way that happens is if you accept that Jesus was the Son of God and that He died for your sins. I believe that if you aren't a child of God, then how can you possibly ever say you truly know love? At least not in the same sense that you now know that God's love equates to the concept of Him always unconditionally giving love to you, no matter what.

To make matters worse, how can we convince others that God lives in us if we, too, aren't at our very core also unconditionally giving love to others? Not to mention the fact that God's love also comes with no strings or conditions attached. Shouldn't this be easy for us to do, also? After all, since God is love, and if He resides in us, then shouldn't we also automatically be able to always unconditionally give love to others, no matter what?

That is just another amazing example of how we all should attempt to learn to achieve Godly love. God is love, so if we don't strive to learn how to love as God loves all of us, then how could we ever really expect to learn to intimately know God? Sounds simple enough, but why is that probably one of the hardest things for any of us to learn, let alone freely do? I have asked myself that question so many times throughout my life. Why does it seem so hard to learn to love as our God already loves us?

There are many excuses we can try to use to make us feel better about why we don't always unconditionally give love to others as our God does. Why? Glad you asked. The main difference between our human understanding of love and what is actually God's love can be summed up in the following statement:

*God's love for us is **unconditional**. God always, freely and unselfishly, "gives love to" all of His children. However, our love is **conditional**. How we choose to "give love to" others is based upon attaching our **feelings** and **emotions** as conditions on how we choose to love them.*

Simply put, we mess up one of the most fundamental truths in all of our relationships after we become children of God. For whatever reason, we choose not to imitate or learn Godly love. We add conditions to how and why we love. Those conditions result when we allow our human emotions and feelings to interfere with always unconditionally giving love to others. Don't you think it's time we stopped the madness? So do I.

The Greatest Gift Ever

Deuteronomy 6:4-5 – "Hear, O Israel! The Lord is our God, the Lord is one! You shall love the Lord your God with all your heart and with all your soul and with all your might." (NASB)

GODLY LOVE

We have already discussed what the greatest gift ever is. We have also explored the differences between God's love and human love. Now then, what is Godly love? "Love" is referred to 818 times in the VOICE version of the Bible, 731 times in the New Revised Standard Version (NRSV) Bible, 759 times in the New Living Translation (NLT) Bible, 686 times in the New International Version (NIV) Bible, 604 times in the New Life Version (NLV) Bible, 500 times in the New King James Version (NKJV) Bible, 484 times in the New American Standard Bible (NASB), and 472 times in the American Standard Version (ASV) Bible (*biblegateway.com*). I believe the best example of the definition of Godly love can be found hidden within 1 Corinthians, Chapter 13, verses 1-8.

Godly Love

1 Corinthians 13:1-3 – "I may be able to speak the languages of men and even of angels, but if I do not have love, it will sound like noisy brass. If I have the gift of speaking God's Word and if I understand all secrets, but do not have love, I am nothing. If I know all things and if I have the gift of faith so I can move mountains, but do not have love, I am nothing. If I give everything I have to feed poor people and if I give my body to be burned, but do not have love, it will not help me." (NLV)

1 Corinthians 13:4-8 – "Love is patient, love is kind. It does not envy, it does not boast, it is not proud. It does not dishonor others, it is not self-seeking, it is not easily angered, it keeps no record of wrongs. Love does not delight in evil but rejoices with the truth. It always protects, always trusts, always hopes, always perseveres. Love never fails. But where there are prophecies, they will cease; where there are tongues, they will be stilled; where there is knowledge, it will pass away." (NIV)

Chances are that you most likely have heard these Bible verses read if you have ever attended a wedding. They are an amazing picture of what God's love for us truly looks like. I believe God revealed His love blueprint to us through these verses. They should certainly become our love blueprint, too. At the very least, they should become our new foundation for how we, too, should strive to always unconditionally give love to others, no matter what. So let's explore them further by breaking these verses down to better comprehend the true meaning behind Godly love and how we, in turn, should begin to transform the way we give love to others.

The first three verses establish the foundation for Godly love by showing us that we could obtain several desired abilities, traits, gifts, and/or possessions. The simple truth of the matter then becomes that we could have all that our hearts could ever desire but, in the end, we become nothing without also having Godly love. Those verses reveal that our faith could even move mountains. However, absent love, our faith also results in having nothing in the end. For some of us, this may not sound like such a challenge. After all, we are human, and we have known how to love for as long as we can remember, right? As ESPN Sportscaster Lee Corso would say, "Not so fast my friend;" unfortunately, there is a lot more.

We might try to fool ourselves into believing that we have this whole love issue down pat, but who are we trying to kid? If we did, we wouldn't be messing up so many of our relationships as much as we have throughout our lives. Luckily, God gave us even more insight into His Godly love blueprint.

Psalm 23:6 – "Surely your goodness and unfailing love will pursue me all the days of my life, and I will live in the house of the Lord forever." (NLT)

1 Corinthians 13:13 – "And now these three remain: faith, hope and love. But the greatest of these is love." (NIV)

Love Is Patient

No, luckily we aren't talking here about you being a medical patient. If you take the time look up definitions of the word *patient*, you might be just as surprised as I was to learn that patient means: capable of bearing or enduring pain, difficulty, provocation, or annoyance with calmness; marked by or exhibiting calm endurance of pain, difficulty, provocation, or annoyance; tolerant, understanding, persevering, constant; not hasty or impulsive (*thefreedictionary.com*).

Okay, now can any of us truly say that defines how they love? Let's not try to fool ourselves any longer. We all know that we refrain from "patiently" enduring situations within our relationships that are uncomfortable or cause us any pain for any lengthy period of time.

Romans 12:12 – "Be joyful in hope, patient in affliction, faithful in prayer." (NIV)

Ephesians 4:2 – "Be completely humble and gentle; be patient, bearing with one another in love." (NIV)

2 Peter 3:9 – "The Lord is not slow about His promise, as some count slowness, but is patient toward you, not wishing for any to perish but for all to come to repentance." (NASB)

We all know, whether consciously or subconsciously, that how we choose to apply our love within a relationship has conditions with an expiration date attached to them. I know mine sure used to. My patience varied from person to person or situation to situation. I wasn't going to patiently waste precious time on unconditionally giving love to another who didn't return it. It was just ridiculous for me to keep wasting my time when I wasn't seeing any return on my investment. Unfortunately, as much as that makes sense to most of us, it couldn't be farther from the truth. We can't put conditions or an expiration date or some sort of time stamp on who we love or for how long we choose to love. If we are truly maturing in our faith, then we must begin to love as God loves us. That means we must transform and show Godly love to others.

To make it even more challenging for us, God called us to patiently love others without attaching any "ifs, ands or buts" to that love, including conditions or expiration dates. We must change our "stinkin thinkin" and adopt God's strategy on how we are going to patiently and unconditionally give love to others from this moment on, no matter what.

I realize that this might be a tough pill for many to swallow. Unfortunately, if you are a child of God and you desire to grow and mature in your faith, then it is something you must begin striving for right here, right now. This is especially true in not just our closest relationships; we must expand that thought process to all of our relationships. We have to begin to patiently and unconditionally give love to others no matter how long it takes us to see any return, if ever, on that investment. God doesn't put "ifs ands or buts" or expiration dates on how He loves us. God loved us before we were born. He loved us when we became His child. God will continue to patiently and unconditionally give love to us, even though at our very core we are all sinners. That, my friend, is a great example of what true Godly love should look like to everyone of us.

Even though we never really earned His love which resulted in our salvation, God will patiently and unconditionally give His love to us from now to eternity. How, then, could we ever become so arrogant to think that we could ever attach our own stipulations to our love by adding things like conditions or expiration dates? "Love Is Patient" translates into no matter how long it takes, no matter what you have to endure, no matter how much it hurts, no matter what the cost, you will always patiently, unconditionally give love to others forever.

How many of our relationships would change for the better if we, too, adopted God's strategy of "Love Is Patient"? Can you imagine the positive change that would be created in your own life if you, too, began to patiently, unconditionally give love to your wife, husband, children, father, mother, family, friends, co-workers, and others, no matter what? Learning to patiently love certainly gives us just a little glimpse of what Godly love for us truly looks like. Not just here on earth, but also most certainly in heaven, as well. Amen!

Unfortunately this whole learning to love as our God loves us will never be easy. It is a process. It is a one-step-at-a-time endeavor that we must choose for ourselves. For some it will be extremely difficult, and for others it might just be a little bit easier. All we can hope for is to do our best and try to emulate Godly love each and every day. It will be a long, slow, sometimes painful journey. No matter what the challenge, no matter what the obstacles, choosing to begin that journey is a huge step in the right direction. Think of all the positives to how your world might change if you began to patiently give love to others. That victory in and of itself should be all the motivation you need to begin to change.

Romans 2:7 – "Whoever has labored diligently and patiently to do what is right—seeking glory, honor, and immortality—God will grant him *endless joy in life eternal*." (VOICE)

Romans 8:25 – "But if we hope for what we do not see, we wait for it with patience." (NRSV)

Love Is Kind

If patience wasn't challenging enough, God expands His love blueprint by adding kindness to the list. Looking up the meaning of kindness I was surprised to learn there were many synonyms associated with that word. Some of the more noteworthy synonyms I discovered were gentleness, generosity, consideration, sympathy, compassion, care, affection, understanding, and hospitality *(google.com)*. So not only must we not put conditions or expiration dates on our love, but we must also show kindness in addition to patience when we always unconditionally give love to others, no matter what. Wow! Some would shout "not fair," and I used to be one of them.

Kindness basically boils down to an act or an action we commit. It comes from within us and transforms itself into existence when we complete an outward act towards someone else. In essence, it

Godly Love

becomes another way for us to "give" to another. As the Hebrew word *ahava* suggests, the greater our act of giving kindness to another, the greater our relationship becomes with the receiver. Here is the kicker: patience and kindness together form that solid foundation we must build in order for us to begin experiencing real Godly love in our lives. Regardless of what the circumstances may be, we are called to be kind as we always unconditionally give love to others, no matter what.

2 Samuel 2:6 – "May the Lord now show you kindness and faithfulness, and I too will show you the same favor because you have done this." (NIV)

Proverbs 3:3 – "Do not let kindness and truth leave you; Bind them around your neck, Write them on the tablet of your heart." (NASB)

Jeremiah 31:3 – "The Lord came to us from far away, saying, I have loved you with a love that lasts forever. So I have helped you come to Me with loving-kindness." (NLV)

2 Corinthians 6:6 – "in purity, in knowledge, in patience, in kindness, in the Holy Spirit, in genuine love," (NASB)

Galatians 5:22-23 – "But the fruit of the Spirit is love, joy, peace, patience, kindness, goodness, faithfulness, gentleness, self-control; against such things there is no law." (NASB)

How many of us can say that we already, always apply kindness in the way we choose to give love to others? If we are being honest with ourselves, I would say the majority of us are kind in our love, depending upon how we feel in the moment. If I am mad, hurt, or upset with someone I know, sometimes I unconsciously — and probably even more so consciously – choose to withhold from giving my love to them. I can't think of any better example than within my own marriage. There were many times when I didn't always unconditionally give love to Lori because I felt she had done "something" to me. Choosing in return not to unconditionally give love to her was my way of evening the score. How childish, if you really think about it. I wasted too much time and effort not always unconditionally giving love to her, no matter what. How much sooner our relationship might have matured into what it is today had I done my part by fulfilling what I was called to do as a Christian husband from the beginning.

If that weren't enough wasted time or effort, I know I also did the same with both my children, Sarah and Robyn. Looking back on it now, I can honestly say that choosing not to love my family as I should have, no matter what, was probably harder in the whole grand scheme of things. My life would have been so much easier had merely I chosen to give them my love despite that fact I felt they had "wronged" me somehow in the first place.

It took way too long for me to finally realize that I was called by God to show Lori and our children what Godly love truly was by always unconditionally giving love to them no matter what. Those of us who call ourselves children of God are also held to this much higher standard. Everything we do and everything we say should be a direct reflection of God's love living inside each of us, regardless of the circumstances. Anything less is unacceptable in God's eyes, and it should be unacceptable in yours as well.

The Greatest Gift Ever

Colossians 3:12 – "As God's chosen ones, holy and beloved, clothe yourselves with compassion, kindness, humility, meekness, and patience." (NRSV)

Love Does Not Envy

As we continue our journey of learning about Godly love, we now come to envy, the next element within God's love blueprint. Envy means having a feeling of discontent and resentment aroused by, and in conjunction with, a desire for the possessions or qualities of another; a feeling of grudging or somewhat admiring discontent aroused by the possessions, achievements, or qualities of another; the desire to have for oneself something possessed by another; covetousness; an object of envy; to feel envy toward (another person); or to regard (something) with envy (*thefreedictionary.com*).

How much does God really know us? So much so that He knew about our inherent desire to "want" the "things" that others had. He knew when He created us that we wouldn't just be satisfied with all He provided us. We always seem to want just a little bit more. Have you ever taken the time to sit down and really think about it? How much time and effort have you wasted wanting something you felt you didn't have? I'm sure your list of those things you felt you wanted were as long as mine was. Instead of being content with all God has provided us, why do we always seem to want what we feel others have that appears to be better than our own? Whether it's living the life of your favorite celebrity, owning that new house like your neighbor has, or desiring that new car your friend just purchased…why does wanting those things seem to consume so much of our time and thoughts? What is it about us that makes us feel that way?

I believe that by adding "Love Does Not Envy" to your list of elements in God's love blueprint that you, too, will soon begin to experience true, Godly love in your life as well. When you start learning to love as our God loves, you will be transformed. The more you change, the more intimate your relationship with God will become. The more intimate your relationship with God becomes, the greater your relationship with your spouse, children, family, friends, or co-workers will become, also.

You, too, in time will notice the change happening inside of you. You will slowly see how you have lost that desire to "covet" those "things" that others have. You will begin to be satisfied with all that God has provided for you. If that isn't motivation enough for you to transform, remember that within the Old Testament under His 10th Commandment, God directs us not to envy.

Exodus 20:17 – "You shall not covet your neighbor's house; you shall not covet your neighbor's wife or his male servant or his female servant or his ox or his donkey or anything that belongs to your neighbor." (NASB)

God tells us not to resent, covet, or desire another person's qualities, attributes, achievements, or possessions. As easy as that commandment is to understand, why does it also seem to be such a stumbling block for so many? What is it inside of us that appears to never be satisfied with all that God has already provided for us, that always feels like we need more of what we believe we don't have? Why do we look at others and feel that our grass isn't as green as the one next door?

Deuteronomy 26:11 – "Then you and the Levites and the foreigners residing among you shall rejoice in all the good things the Lord your God has given to you and your household." (NIV)

Proverbs 14:30 – "A heart at peace gives life to the body, but envy rots the bones." (NIV)

    This is the bottom line: happy is the one who wants what he has, and unhappy is the one who wants what he doesn't have. This part of the whole Godly love puzzle was so important to God that not only did He make it part of His love blueprint, but it was also part of His original Ten Commandments. What does this mean for us? It means be satisfied and content with **everything** God gives you. No matter how green another's lawn may appear, in the end it is still just grass. If you want your grass to be greener, then you must water your own lawn, and let your neighbors worry about watering theirs.

    We are all part of God's bigger plan. God made you the way you are and provided you with the many things He did because that is what He wanted for you. Your particular situation and circumstances are how you fit into God's plans. God made all of us in His own image. He wanted you to look the way you do for a reason. God gave you certain spiritual

The Greatest Gift Ever

gifts because He wanted you to have them. If you are His child, you married whom you did because it was His plan. In short, all that we have is because God wanted us to have it, and since it all came from God, be happy, content, and satisfied with all God has provided for you.

If you waste your time wishing for the other things God didn't give you but gave to others, then you aren't following God's plan for you. If you aren't following God's plan for your life, how could you ever hope to learn what Godly love is by always unconditionally giving love to others? If you aren't frustrated enough yet, hold on and keep reading. It gets so much better!

Psalm 119:35 – "Make me walk along the path of your commands, for that is where my happiness is found." (NLT)

James 3:16 – "For where you have envy and selfish ambition, there you find disorder and every evil practice." (NIV)

Godly Love

Love Does Not Boast

This part of God's love blueprint may seem a little confusing to some; it was for me, at first. If we consider the context in which the word "boast" was used in the Bible, then boasting means "to praise." In essence, boasting is something you say or do. It becomes another example of an outward act on our part.

Ephesians 1:3-5 – "All praise to God, the Father of our Lord Jesus Christ, who has blessed us with every spiritual blessing in the heavenly realms because we are united with Christ. Even before he made the world, God loved us and chose us in Christ to be holy and without fault in his eyes. God decided in advance to adopt us into his own family by bringing us to himself through Jesus Christ. This is what he wanted to do, and it gave him great pleasure." (NLT)

How does this fit into God's love blueprint? When you don't praise God for everything He has given you but instead praise yourself for all your achievements, then you are boasting the wrong way. If you give credit to yourself instead of where credit is due, then you are improperly boasting. I think it even goes a little further to include boasting about how much "better" you, your family, your job, or your life is compared to others. Learning "to praise" God for everything you have should become your goal.

Psalm 44:8 – "O God, we give glory to you all day long and constantly praise your name." (NLT)

Psalm 149:1,3-4 – "Praise the Eternal! *Write* new songs; sing them to Him *with all your might*! Gather with His faithful followers in *joyful* praise; So *let the music begin*; praise His name—dance and sing to *the rhythm of* the tambourine, and *to the tune of* the harp. For the Eternal *is listening,* and nothing pleases Him more than His people; He raises up the poor and endows them with His salvation." (VOICE)

If you are a child of God and speak, brag, or make public that you are the reason behind all of your abilities, achievements, or accomplishments instead of God being the reason, then you are not showing others what Godly love truly looks like. Giving God all the credit is the proper way for you to boast. Anything other than that is unacceptable within God's whole love blueprint.

One of the best examples I can think of that doesn't reflect Godly love has become very rampant in our society today. How many of us can point to someone we know whose social media page is nothing more than a boast about how great they believe their life is or at least how it all appears to be? They claim that all their accomplishments or achievements are because of what they did. They don't rightly give all the credit like they should to God.

What about those professional athletes we watch on television? Those who give glory to God for all their talents or accomplishments have their heads and hearts in the right place. As we have seen, giving God credit for all we have is the right way to boast about God. If you are doing anything else, then you need to shift gears and try instead to give all the credit where it is due.

Psalm 94:4 – "They pour out their arrogant words; all the evildoers boast." (NRSV)

1 Corinthians 1:29-31 – "As a result, no one can ever boast in the presence of God. God has united you with Christ Jesus. For our benefit God made him to be wisdom itself. Christ made us right with God; he made us pure and holy, and he freed us from sin. Therefore, as the Scriptures say, 'If you want to boast, boast only about the Lord.'" (NLT)

Love Is Not Proud

God places "proud" as the next element in His Godly love blueprint. There are several definitions for proud. The ones I believe that most apply to better understanding Godly love are feeling pleasurable satisfaction over an act, possession, quality, or relationship by which one measures one's stature or self-worth; and filled with or showing excessive self-esteem *(thefreedictionary.com)*.

You can see some similarities between boasting and pride. However, the main difference between them is that boasting involves an outward act committed by us, such as bragging about our achievements; conversely, pride involves having a mindset – an internal attitude — that you are better than others. Either way, pride that you are somehow better than others for any reason isn't the true reflection of Godly love that you should strive for.

Philippians 2:5-8 – "In other words, adopt the mind-set of Jesus the Anointed. Live with His attitude in your hearts. Remember: Though He was in the form of God, He chose not to cling to equality with God; But He poured Himself out to fill a vessel brand new; a servant in form and a man indeed. The very likeness of humanity, He humbled Himself, obedient to death—a merciless death on the cross!" (VOICE)

Humility is the very core attribute that God wants all of His children to posses when it comes to learning how to always unconditionally give love to others. Without humility, you will continually stumble, because boasting and pride will always get in the way. Our ultimate goal, then, should be to replace both boasting and pride with humility.

Deuteronomy 8:14 – "…be careful not to become proud. Do not forget the Lord your God Who brought you out of the land of Egypt, out of the house where you were servants." (NLV)

Psalm 31:23 – "Love the Lord, all his faithful people! The Lord preserves those who are true to him, but the proud he pays back in full." (NIV)

Proverbs 16:5 – "Everyone who is proud in heart is an abomination to the Lord; Assuredly, he will not be unpunished." (NASB)

Romans 12:16 – "Live in harmony with each other. Don't be too proud to enjoy the company of ordinary people. And don't think you know it all!" (NLT)

Having the mindset that God is responsible for everything that we are reflects the proper type of pride we should possess within the confines of God's love blueprint. With that as a foundation, we are then able to show others true Godly love, because we aren't allowing our pride to interfere with how or when we would choose to always unconditionally give love to others. Think of it like this: without our pride attached to love, we would always unconditionally give love to others, because God's love lives and flows within us. We would then freely give things like instant forgiveness without letting our pride get in the way. Love with humility but without pride is how God already loves each one of His children.

Shouldn't we, too, strive to leave our pride out of how we love and choose to be humble, instead? How many unnecessary differences of opinions do we experience in a lifetime when we allow our pride to come into play? I can think of many such circumstances between just Lori and me. But what about those instances where you hear about family members not speaking to one another for years because their pride won't allow them to simply apologize? How many times have we allowed pride to come between our call to always unconditionally give love to others? More times than we will admit, I'm sure.

1 Samuel 2:3 – "Speak no more in your pride. Do not let proud talk come out of your mouth. For the Lord is a God Who knows. Actions are weighed by Him." (NLV)

2 Chronicles 7:14 – "…if my people, who are called by my name, will humble themselves and pray and seek my face and turn from their wicked ways, then I will hear from heaven, and I will forgive their sin and will heal their land." (NIV)

Matthew 23:12 – "Whoever exalts himself shall be humbled; and whoever humbles himself shall be exalted." (NASB)

James 4:10 – "Humble yourselves before the Lord, and He will lift you up." (NIV)

1 Peter 5:6 – "Therefore humble yourselves under the mighty hand of God, that He may exalt you at the proper time, …" (NASB)

Love Does Not Dishonor Others

As we continue along our journey into better comprehending Godly love, we are next faced with the concept of not dishonoring others as another element of God's love blueprint. Simply put, to dishonor others means to somehow bring disgrace, shame, or humiliation upon someone. As with some of the previous foundational elements, dishonoring someone requires us to commit an outward act towards the receiver. We must outwardly disgrace, shame, or humiliate another.

Is it totally embarrassing that you could ever be capable of doing anything like that, now that you have a much clearer picture of what true Godly love looks like? Think about it. How could we ever be capable of doing such a thing to someone else? To make matters worse, we bring them dishonor, and then even have the boldness to declare that we love them on top of it all. My initial human response would be to say thanks, but no thanks. How about you?

So then on the flip side, to honor someone means to "give" them the recognition, the glory, or the credit for some exceptional achievement. Honoring someone also means holding them in high esteem or simply just respecting them.

Romans 12:10 – "Be devoted to one another in love. Honor one another above yourselves." (NIV)

As with envy, God saw fit to further expand His original Ten Commandments to include not dishonoring others in His love blueprint. In its truest form, honoring someone means having high respect for them or holding someone in high esteem. It can also be viewed from the angle that honoring others involves fulfilling an agreement or contract with them. How appropriate that God would make that a stipulation within His love blueprint. What else could ever be more reflecting of Godly love than honoring your wife, your husband, and your marriage vows?

I don't know what your wedding vows may have looked like but, since Lori and I eloped, our vows were a little more traditional. They were along the lines of "I take thee to be my lawful wedded husband/wife, to have and to hold, from this day forward, for better, for worse, for richer, for poorer, in sickness and in health, forsaking all others, to love and to cherish, till death do us part." It's amazing how different those very same wedding vows now appear after looking at them through our new Godly love lenses. With a much clearer understanding of what God's love looks like, is there any better way for me to honor Lori than by fulfilling my obligations to her that were contained within our marriage vows? Based upon what we've learned so far, I would definitely have to say no. Yet, sadly, I dishonor her each time I fail to uphold those same vows that we made to each other in God's presence.

If that doesn't grab your attention, then I don't know what else will. Our new insight into what Godly love is compels us to always unconditionally give love to others; this now includes honoring others by fulfilling our agreements with them. The best example we were given of how a couple can honor each other was in the case of their marriage vows. It can't be said any simpler than that.

Godly Love

Ephesians 5:28-31 – "So men should love their wives as they love their own bodies. He who loves his wife loves himself. No man hates himself. He takes care of his own body. That is the way Christ does. He cares for His body which is the church. We are all a part of His body, the church. For this reason, a man must leave his father and mother when he gets married and be joined to his wife. The two become one." (NLV)

Armed with our new knowledge and insight into true Godly love, aren't we now forced to consider how we must apply this love to our everyday lives? How will God's love impact our world? How many families would be a lot better off if husbands, wives, and children were honoring one another? How many couples would still be together today if both parties were "giving" honor to the other by fulfilling their marriage vows? How many needless, angry thoughts or statements wouldn't we think or say if we were honoring our family, friends, or co-workers? What would our world look like today if God's children were always unconditionally giving love to others just by simply honoring one another? I don't know about you, but I'm thinking along the lines of what Heaven on Earth might truly start to look like.

Proverbs 3:35 – "*In the end,* the wise will receive honor, but fools will face humiliation." (VOICE)

Proverbs 11:2 – "When pride comes, then comes dishonor, But with the humble is wisdom." (NASB)

Hebrews 13:4 – "Marriage should be honored by all, and the marriage bed kept pure, for God will judge the adulterer and all the sexually immoral." (NIV)

Love Is Not Self-Seeking

To be self-seeking means to be concerned with fulfilling your own goals or interests. Self-seeking at its very core is the truest form of selfishness. As contained within some of the other Godly love blueprint elements, self-seeking comes from inside of us and is more like a state of mind or an attitude we display towards others. Self-seeking goes against the very foundation of God's love blueprint. Godly love requires us to always unconditionally give love to others, no matter what, and self-seeking goes against that same requirement. If we are failing to "give" in our loving, then we don't love in the first place. You can't be self-seeking and say you love another. The two concepts are polar opposites. They can't exist together in Godly love.

Some of the more common synonyms associated with self-seeking are being prideful, boasting, conceited, pompous, and vain. Do any of those words convey any form of the Godly love we have learned about? I didn't think so, either. Surprisingly, the main antonym that self-seeking has in common with pride is humble. Are you starting to get a better idea of what is and what isn't Godly love?

Romans 13:14 – "Instead, wrap yourselves in the Lord Jesus, God's Anointed, and do not fuel your sinful imagination by indulging *your self-seeking desire* for the pleasures of the flesh." (VOICE)

I am ashamed to admit that this was one of my biggest struggles when it came to finally understanding what Godly love was, instead of what I believed love was. It all went back to my inability to refrain from attaching my emotions and feelings to how I chose to give love to others. This was never more evident in my life, especially during the early years of my marriage, than how I chose to give my love to Lori. If she wasn't giving me something in return after I somehow gave her my love, then she didn't really love me, or so I was led to believe.

Our very world teaches us to be self-seeking, to put our needs in front of others needs. How many times have we heard our world telling us, "it's all about me?" But if we are truly children of God, then we wouldn't ever need to be self-seeking, because we would be too busy always unconditionally giving love to others. We wouldn't be consumed with trying to fulfill our own goals or our own interests because we wouldn't have any. Our goals and interests would only consist of trying to fulfill the goals or the interests of those we are giving love to.

The hardest part of understanding this from human eyes goes back to the Greek word *agape* and Hebrew word *ahava*. In Christianity, agape describes the love God has for you and you for Him. Remember, in the ahava concept, our relationship grows stronger with another person when we are continually "giving" our love to them.

Unfortunately, our world teaches us to do the exact opposite. We are misguided and led to believe

Godly Love

that in order for us to obtain true love, we need to find the one who will make us happy and fulfill all of our dreams. You will become more mature in your faith and your relationship with God will grow so much stronger once you put your self-seeking aside. Godly love requires us to put aside all of our own goals and desires. It is crucial that you begin to always unconditionally give love to others by putting them first and you second. That, my friend, is how you keep from allowing your love to ever become self-seeking in the first place.

Romans 2:8-10 – "But for those who are self-seeking and who reject the truth and follow evil, there will be wrath and anger. There will be trouble and distress for every human being who does evil: first for the Jew, then for the Gentile; but glory, honor and peace for everyone who does good: first for the Jew, then for the Gentile." (NIV)

James 3:14 – "But if you have bitter envy and self-seeking in your hearts, do not boast and lie against the truth." (NKJV)

Love Is Not Easily Angered

Anger is the next hurdle we have to overcome to better understand the whole concept of Godly love. Anger is literally one of mankind's worst emotions. Anger can be defined as a strong feeling of displeasure or hostility; to be enraged or provoked; a feeling of great annoyance or antagonism as a result of some real or perceived grievance *(thefreedictionary. com)*. Some of the notable synonyms for anger are rage, fury, resentment, and wrath.

If we are being honest with ourselves, I'm sure we would all agree that we are less than perfect when it comes to the subject of anger. Under God's love blueprint, we would not be easily provoked, resentful, aggravated, or irritated with someone if we are always unconditionally giving love to them. Our ultimate goal under Godly love is, instead, to be slow to anger.

If you take the time to step back from the situation that is causing you to feel angry and analyze it, chances are that something else is causing you to be angry — and it's not necessarily your loved one. Unfortunately, as the old saying goes, we take our anger out on our loved ones. If you are applying the concepts of *agape* or *ahava* to that relationship, how can you ever allow your loved one to easily upset or anger you if you are "giving" love to them in the first place? If you are always unconditionally giving love to them, then the simple truth is that you can't allow them to anger you–ever! It goes against the very foundation of God's love blueprint. Anger can only exist when you are failing to uphold your end of God's whole love plan for your life.

Psalm 145:8 – "The Lord is gracious and merciful; Slow to anger and great in lovingkindness." (NASB)

Proverbs 14:29 – "People with understanding control their anger; a hot temper shows great foolishness." (NLT)

Proverbs 15:1 – "A gentle answer deflects anger, but harsh words make tempers flare." (NLT)

Proverbs 29:11 – "A fool gives full vent to anger, but the wise quietly holds it back." (NRSV)

As part of that church future leadership course I previously discussed, one of the books I read was

Craig and Amy Groeschel's book, *From This Day Forward: Five Commitments to Fail-Proof Your Marriage*. I strongly encourage you to read this book as an additional resource. For me, this book became Marriage 101. In it I learned many new ways to handle conflict and other situations that Lori and I have experienced over the years. One of my favorites became a rule I now live by. Before I said anything to Lori that might "anger" her, I first had to ask myself two questions. First, "Does what I am thinking need to be said?" Second, "Does what I am thinking need to be said right now?" Ladies and Gentlemen, all I can say is, man, does that really work. There have been so many unnecessary arguments that I have avoided with Lori by stopping first to answer those two questions before opening my big mouth. I challenge you to try it out for yourself. See if it makes as significant an impact on your marriage that it has on mine. You have nothing to lose. More often than not, I know it will help keep you from becoming easily angered, and it will also certainly help your loved ones from the same.

Galatians 5:19-21 – "When you follow the desires of your sinful nature, the results are very clear: sexual immorality, impurity, lustful pleasures, idolatry, sorcery, hostility, quarreling, jealousy, outbursts of anger, selfish ambition, dissension, division, envy, drunkenness, wild parties, and other sins like these. Let me tell you again, as I have before, that anyone living that sort of life will not inherit the Kingdom of God." (NLT)

Ephesians 4:26 – "Be ANGRY, AND *YET* DO NOT SIN; do not let the sun go down on your anger, …" (NASB)

Ephesians 4:31 – "Let all bitterness and wrath and anger and clamor and slander be put away from you, along with all malice." (NASB)

Colossians 3:8 – "But now you must also rid yourselves of all such things as these: anger, rage, malice, slander, and filthy language from your lips." (NIV)

Hebrews 12:15 – "See to it that no one falls short of the grace of God and that no bitter root grows up to cause trouble and defile many." (NIV)

James 1:19-20 – "My Christian brothers, you know everyone should listen much and speak little. He should be slow to become angry. A man's anger does not allow him to be right with God." (NLV)

Love Keeps No Record of Wrongs

This part of God's whole love blueprint is my favorite. I believe that this statement stands on its own and needs no further explanation of its definition. Point blank, we don't dwell on the wrongs we believe others have done to us. A "wrong" in and of itself would be all the things we do that go against what we now know to be Godly love.

Just as God does for each one of us, once we confess our sins to Him, we are instantly forgiven and they are forgotten. God doesn't write them all down somewhere. He doesn't keep track of them to see how well you are doing along your Christian journey. God doesn't keep score. He doesn't throw it back in your face or occasionally remind you about it. Nope, God always, unconditionally continues to give love to us, no matter what. We must also learn to do the same.

Did you catch all those very important points? To record something would require God to write down all of your wrongs and maintain a permanent account

Godly Love

of your performance somewhere. Expanding your understanding just a little bit further, let's refer to a "wrong" as an action by you that, according to Godly love, is viewed as improper, immoral, unjust, inappropriate, unfaithful, or disloyal. In short, Godly love doesn't keep a record of your sins after you have confessed them to God and asked for forgiveness. Can you imagine what that permanent account of your wrongs would look like if God wrote them all down somewhere and kept track? Does anyone believe they would receive a passing score? Godly love consists of instant forgiveness for all of our sins once we have confessed them to God and, thankfully, He doesn't also keep track of them all, either.

Psalm 103:11-13 – "*Measure* how high heaven is above the earth; God's *wide,* loving, kind heart is greater for those who revere Him. *You see,* God takes *all* our crimes—*our seemingly inexhaustible sins*—and removes them. As far as east is from the west, *He removes them* from us. An *earthly* father expresses love for his children; it is no different *with our heavenly Father;* The Eternal shows His love for those who revere Him." (VOICE)

Why does it seem so hard for us to apply that same concept to how and why we love the way we do, as well? Could it have something to do with attaching our feelings and emotions to the way we choose to love? I'm sure if you looked at yourself in the mirror and asked yourself those very same questions, the answers you discover staring you right back in the face reveal that you still have a long way to go to learn how to always unconditionally give love to others, no matter what.

Life is way too short to keep remembering or dwelling on past events, situations, or circumstances where we believe we were wronged. Besides, if we are so consumed with always unconditionally giving love to others, then how could we ever possibly have time to focus our attention on any of their wrongs? As embarrassing as that is, it is exactly what we do the majority of the time.

I know I, for one, am guilty as charged. Far too often throughout my own life, I can point to numerous occasions when, instead of displaying Godly love by leaving the past in the past, I chose instead to keep a record of a wrong I perceived someone had done to me. Not only did I keep a record of it, but I also dwelled on it. I allowed that record of wrong to consume my time, my thoughts, my energy, and my emotions.

As hard as that story may seem for some, I have another point that I doubt you're going to be happy with, either. I believe that a real measure of how we are truly beginning to transform into showing others Godly love lies within our ability to instantly forgive someone of a perceived wrong, right on the spot, no matter what. Easier said than done, right? Wouldn't that ability make our Christian journey that much better? Should children of God really struggle with the concept of instant forgiveness? Why? Does God really ever give us a choice to withhold our forgiveness towards others in the first place?

Matthew 6:12 – "'And forgive us our debts, as we also have forgiven our debtors." (NASB)

Matthew 6:14-15 – "For if you forgive other people when they sin against you, your heavenly Father will also forgive you. But if you do not forgive others their sins, your Father will not forgive your sins." (NIV)

Mark 11:25 – "And when you stand praying, if you hold anything against anyone, forgive them, so that your Father in heaven may forgive you your sins." (NIV)

Luke 6:37 – "Do not judge, and you will not be judged. Do not condemn, and you will not be condemned. Forgive, and you will be forgiven." (NIV)

Ephesians 4:32 – "Instead, be kind to each other, tenderhearted, forgiving one another, just as God through Christ has forgiven you." (NLT)

This is not something we have learned to do so easily, is it? It goes against many of the worldly ideas we've learned during our entire lives. This has been a huge obstacle for me to overcome. I realize now how futile it was to try to keep track of all the wrongs done to me, which never took me to a very good place, anyway. Being angry and holding back my forgiveness never served any good purpose — it just made me more angry, bitter, and depressed. Not to mention that, looking back on it now, I realize it was a huge waste of time. I know it was also an enormous stumbling block not only to my ability to grow closer with God but also to intimacy with those closest to me. So I am encouraged that we, too, can learn to always, unconditionally give love to others by not keeping records of wrongs, no matter what.

What a great example God gives us as a model in Luke 15:11-32 when Jesus used the Parable of the Lost Son. If that isn't motivation enough for us to change, consider God's gift of our salvation through the sacrifice of His son, Jesus. God loved you so much that he "gave" His son so you, too, would be forgiven of all your wrongs and have eternal life with Him. If God kept a record of your wrongs, would you ever truly deserve your salvation? I think you all already know the answer to that question.

Who will ever forget how God's love was clearly demonstrated by the Amish community when they instantly forgave the gunman after the tragic West Nickel Mines School shooting on October 2, 2006? Even more inspirational are the stories we often hear about when people have forgiven others who were responsible for killing their loved ones. We might not always see "instant" forgiveness in our own lives, but these stories are worth noting because, in the end, people chose to unconditionally give love to others by forgiving instead of keeping a record of wrongs. The woman who inspired Matthew West's song, "Forgiveness," also chose to forgive. It might have not been instantly, but she did eventually forgive. As a result, we see not only how forgiveness transformed her but also how her forgiveness changed the offenders' life, as well.

How arrogant are we if we expect instant forgiveness from God after we confess our sins but then refuse to also instantly forgive others? What do you expect from another after they say "I'm sorry"? Does withholding your forgiveness for some time so they can feel guilty longer make you feel any better in the end? Are they supposed to say sorry more than once before you feel obliged to forgive? Do you expect them to not keep a record of your wrongs? Are you often reoffended if you don't hear "I forgive you" immediately after your apology? Come on, be honest.

Before putting the material for this book together, Lori and I attended a Matthew West concert in Lancaster, PA. During his show, Matthew talked about how love keeps no record of wrong. I had never really thought about that aspect of Godly love until that very from God "ah ha" moment. It made perfect sense to me and was one of the motivating factors behind my beginning to better understand God's love blueprint. That whole lesson inspired me to paint those very words that "Love Keeps No Records of Wrong" on a wooden box. That box now strategically sits within our home as a constant reminder for us to keep the past in the past and not dwell on it.

Psalm 32:1 – "How blessed is he whose transgression is forgiven, whose sin is covered!" (NASB)

Psalm 130:4 – "But with you there is forgiveness, so that we can, with reverence, serve you." (NIV)

Matthew 18:21 – "Then Peter came to Jesus and asked, 'Lord, how many times shall I forgive my brother or sister who sins against me? Up to seven times?' " (NIV)

Luke 7:47 – "For this reason I say to you, her sins, which are many, have been forgiven, for she loved much; but he who is forgiven little, loves little." (NASB)

Romans 12:19 – "Christian brothers, never pay back someone for the bad he has done to you. Let the anger of God take care of the other person. The

Holy Writings say, 'I will pay back to them what they should get, says the Lord.' "(NLV)

Romans 4:7 – "Blessed are those whose transgressions are forgiven, whose sins are covered." (NIV)

1 Thessalonians 5:15 – "Make sure that nobody pays back wrong for wrong, but always strive to do what is good for each other and for everyone else." (NIV)

Love Does Not Delight In Evil

As with all of these elements of God's love blueprint, this one became very interesting to me the more I thought about it. Looking at love from this perspective helped me to understand it more clearly. To delight means you experience great pleasure, joy, extreme satisfaction or that you receive great enjoyment from something. Adding "evil" to the definition, it then becomes something that is morally bad or wrong; wicked; causing injury, destruction, or pain; harmful; characterized by anger or spite; or malicious (*thefreedictionary.com*). Combining the two ideas shows that delighting in evil means you find pleasure, joy, happiness, or that you're charmed, thrilled, or even captivated by immoral, wicked, sinful, destructive, malicious, or dishonorable acts.

How could a child of God ever be capable of delighting in evil? Doesn't the very notion of evil contradict the very foundation of your Christian beliefs? Evil exists because Satan has been trying to lure you into living apart from God from the very beginning. Delighting in evil is not part of Godly love and has no place within God's whole love blueprint.

God wants no barriers between Him and you, but Satan does. God doesn't make you feel unworthy of His love and the gift of your salvation. We place those barriers between God and ourselves because we allow Satan to cast doubt and fear into our lives. If we're living in harmony with God and submit ourselves to Him, how could Satan ever gain a foothold in our lives to create those areas where we have doubt and fear? God is always in control and has a perfect plan for each one of us. When we allow Satan to enter into the picture, we soon discover we have allowed ourselves to be blown off course. It is exactly during those times when you're in the midst of stormy seas that you must take your hands off the wheel and allow God to bring you back on course.

Don't allow Satan to gain the foothold he needs to separate you from God. Keep your eyes on the prize.

1 Samuel 12:20 – "Do not be afraid," Samuel replied. "You have done all this evil; yet do not turn away from the Lord, but serve the Lord with all your heart." (NIV)

2 Chronicles 12:14 – "He did evil because he did not set his heart to seek the Lord." (NASB)

Psalm 34:13-14 – "...keep your tongue from evil and your lips from telling lies. Turn from evil and do good; seek peace and pursue it." (NIV)

Proverbs 11:19 – "He who is steadfast in righteousness *will attain* to life, And he who pursues evil *will bring about* his own death." (NASB)

The word "evil" can be found 430 times in the NIV Bible, 491 times in the NKJV Bible, 510 times in the NASB, 512 times in the VOICE Bible, 530 times in the NLT Bible, 580 times in the NRSV Bible, and 626 times in the ASV Bible (*biblegateway.com*). Suffice it to say that this aspect of God's love blueprint speaks for itself. As a child of God, you're called to refrain from evil and to resist committing evil acts, because you're always, unconditionally giving love to others, no matter what.

Psalm 97:10 – "You who love the Lord, hate evil! He protects the lives of his godly people and rescues them from the power of the wicked." (NLT)

Matthew 9:4 – "But Jesus, knowing their thoughts, said, 'Why do you think evil in your hearts?' " (NKJV)

Romans 12:9 – "Love others *well, and* don't hide behind a mask; love authentically. Despise evil; pursue what is good *as if your life depends on it*." (VOICE)

God's love indwells inside of you after you join His family. You were changed after you were saved. Your mind, heart, and soul should now be focused only on Godly things, not on anything evil from the world you left behind. If you're walking in harmony with God, then you should find it extremely difficult to ever delight in evil. You should always turn from evil and run as fast as you can away from it. Evil has not, and never will, have a place within Godly love.

James 1:21 – "Therefore, get rid of all moral filth and the evil that is so prevalent and humbly accept the word planted in you, which can save you." (NIV)

1 John 2:15-16 – "Do not love the world nor the things in the world. If anyone loves the world, the love of the Father is not in him. For all that is in the world, the lust of the flesh and the lust of the eyes and the boastful pride of life, is not from the Father, but is from the world." (NASB)

3 John 1:11 – "Dear friend, do not imitate what is evil but what is good. Anyone who does what is good is from God. Anyone who does what is evil has not seen God." (NIV)

Love Rejoices in the Truth

"Rejoicing" refers to our ability to experience joy or delight towards or in something. The meaning of truth within the Godly love blueprint is something we accept as true, or factual. When Godly love and truth combine, our new understanding as a child of God, based on our new self in Christ, can establish our faith and belief in love and truth. Believing in

Godly Love

the truth of God's love simply means that you have faith that it is true love. When always, unconditionally giving love to others, it isn't enough to just practice it; you must also delight in doing so, because you have faith that Godly love is the only true and proper way to show love to others.

Sound too complicated? It isn't. With your new Godly love lenses, do you now understand how differently God's love should appear to you? God added rejoicing in the truth as another element in His Godly love blueprint, because He wanted you to find joy and have faith in the fact that His love for you is the greatest truth there is.

John 3:16 – "For God so loved the world that he gave his only Son, so that everyone who believes in him may not perish but may have eternal life." (NRSV)

Not only should we constantly rejoice in knowing the truth of God's love for us, but we also should delight in knowing the truth about how we, too, should always, unconditionally choose to give love to others, no matter what. That rejoicing should consume and overwhelm you. You should always be shouting and boasting every day because of your

The Greatest Gift Ever

new knowledge. Apply it correctly and your faith, too, will reach new heights as you allow yourself to become delightedly consumed with that same truth about Godly love.

After all, isn't the very foundation of our Christian faith based upon our belief in the truth that God unconditionally gave His love to us by sacrificing His son Jesus so we would live with Him forever? With that as our faith's foundation, one of our main goals then becomes maturing in our faith so that we, too, can become more Christ-like in our own journey with God. Unfortunately, that maturity comes at a cost to every one of Christ's followers. That cost is the realization that you're now called upon to always, unconditionally give love to others, no matter what.

1 John 3:18 – "My children, let us not love with words or in talk only. Let us love by what we do and in truth." (NLV)

Our ability to always, unconditionally give love to others comes from inside us by way of the indwelling Holy Spirit Who dwells within us. Because we are children of God, then what "comes" out from inside of us should always reflect to others that God's love resonates within each one of us all of the time, no matter what. Colton Dixon's song, "Let Them See You in Me," is a great way to ponder what Godly love inside each one of us should always look like to others.

Your journey going forward with this new knowledge won't be easy. Every day will be challenging. You will be constantly under attack by Satan and all that is in our world that goes against your belief in God. The easy way out is to quit or to even refuse trying to change. The right thing to do is to try your best each day. Your goal should be to take one day at a time. Choose to make a difference in this world by showing others what always, unconditionally giving love to others, no matter what, looks like. If at first you don't succeed one day, wake up the next day by choosing to shake off yesterday's failures, and don't lose hope in your ultimate goal. Keep your eyes focused on the prize. Slowly, over time, each day will become a little easier than the last. Before you know it, you'll be well on your way to maturing into the Christian God created you to be in the first place.

Deuteronomy 28:2 – "And all these blessings shall come upon you and overtake you, because you obey the voice of the Lord your God: ..." (NKJV)

Psalm 119:160 – "The sum of Your word is truth, And every one of Your righteous ordinances is everlasting." (NASB)

John 14:21 – "They who have my commandments and keep them are those who love me; and those who love me will be loved by my Father, and I will love them and reveal myself to them." (NRSV)

1 Peter 1:22 – "You have made your souls pure by obeying the truth through the Holy Spirit. This has given you a true love for the Christians. Let it be a true love from the heart." (NLV)

Love Always Protects

Protection translates into providing another with a shield, cover, or by keeping them safe from harm or injury. Protection has always been one of mankind's most basic physical needs. If we are protecting or shielding another from harm, then how could we ever harm or injure anyone if we are always, unconditionally giving love to them, no matter what? In the context of agape or ahava, our whole relationship is based upon growing closer together by constantly giving to that relationship. I don't know about you, but harming others goes against the basic fundamentals of being a Christian. God instilled in us the desire to provide protection to others. As such, this aspect of God's love should come naturally to us all. Shouldn't this become the easiest part of our whole transformation to complete?

Yet we often choose not to protect others, because we attach our conditions, expiration dates, emotions, and feelings. Instead, we should provide protection to all because we better understand that we are called to always, unconditionally give love to others, no matter what. The best example of Godly love protection is in the following Bible verse:

John 15:12-14 – "My commandment to you is this: love others as I have loved you. There is no greater way to love than to give your life for your friends. You celebrate our friendship if you obey this command." (VOICE)

By adhering to God's love blueprint, we not only receive protection from God because He loves us, but we also must protect others, too. "Always" is defined as, at all times; for all time; forever; at any time; and in any event *(thefreedictionary.com)*. Wow! Your expanded understanding of God's love blueprint, which specifies that love always protects, lets you now see that you're called to shield others at all times, forever, at any time, or in any event. If you want to transform, then you can no longer hold onto your previous worldly concept of love. You must apply each new aspect of God's love blueprint to your life right here, right now, not just when it suits you best or fits into your plans. You need to begin to always, unconditionally give love to others by protecting them all the time, no matter what.

Psalm 5:11 – "But let all who take refuge in you be glad; let them ever sing for joy. Spread your protection over them, that those who love your name may rejoice in you." (NIV)

Psalm 40:11 – "Lord, don't hold back your tender mercies from me. Let your unfailing love and faithfulness always protect me." (NLT)

Psalm 91:14 – "The Lord says, 'I will rescue those who love me. I will protect those who trust in my name.' " (NLT)

Proverbs 3:26 – "For the Eternal is always there to protect you. He will safeguard your each and every step." (VOICE)

Proverbs 30:5 – "Every word of God proves true. He is a shield to all who come to him for protection." (NLT)

2 Thessalonians 3:3 – "But the Lord is faithful, and he will strengthen you and protect you from the evil one." (NIV)

Love Always Trusts

Now we come to what I believe is one of the more challenging elements within God's whole love blueprint. To have trust means you place confidence in, depend upon, believe in, or hope in someone or something. As with protecting, God makes this concept tougher to grasp by adding the stipulation of "always" to the mix. Always trusting love means you place confidence in Godly love forever, no matter what. Does that typically reflect the level of trust you already know lies inside of you? Do you forever believe that God's love will make your future turn out brighter? Is your trust in God exemplified by you choosing to always, unconditionally give love to others, no matter what? If you're being honest, I'm sure you've already figured out the correct answer to those questions.

We have all been hurt or felt wronged by someone else at various times in our lives. I know from my own experiences that my level of trust towards others was significantly impacted when they hurt me. As hard as that is for us to deal with, the reality, more often than not, becomes that those closest to us seem to also be the ones who hurt us the most and, unfortunately, probably more than once. Even harder than that to admit might even be the fact that we, too, are also responsible for hurting or wronging others in our lives. Those we typically hurt most often are also probably those who we are closest to. All the "negative" feelings we bury inside as a result of those bad experiences have probably led us to not trust others at some point in our lives. Is it ever okay for us not to trust?

Godly Love

Unfortunately, we know it isn't, especially since we have already learned that Godly love keeps no record of wrongs. Always trusting means that you will stand firm in your belief in another's reliability or character, no matter what. To properly emulate Godly love, we must always, unconditionally give love to others by always trusting them, no matter how many times they have revealed they weren't trustworthy to begin with by their past actions.

I know that sounds harsh, and before I began studying God's love blueprint, it sounded harsh to me, too. Doesn't that reality go against all that we learned from the world by attaching our emotions and feelings to how we love in the first place? Where is my "bang for the buck?" Why should I invest giving my love to someone who has repeatedly proven untrustworthy? Why should I remain in a relationship in which my loved one has constantly broken my trust? Our list of "what ifs" could become as endless as our excuses for choosing not to forever place trust in those who have hurt us. Ultimately, you're forced to look at God's love blueprint to "always trust" from this perspective. Doesn't God consistently give you His trust, no matter what? God always, unconditionally gives His love to you

The Greatest Gift Ever

despite your untrustworthiness that is always due to your very nature to sin.

Psalm 9:10 – "Those who know your name trust in you, for you, O Lord, do not abandon those who search for you." (NLT)

Psalm 13:5 – "But I have trusted in Your lovingkindness; My heart shall rejoice in Your salvation." (NASB)

Psalm 25:1 – "In you, Lord my God, I put my trust." (NIV)

Psalm 28:7 – "The Lord is my strength and my shield; my heart trusts in him, and he helps me. My heart leaps for joy, and with my song I praise him." (NIV)

Psalm 62:8 – "Trust in Him at all times, O people; Pour out your heart before Him; God is a refuge for us." (NASB)

Proverbs 3:5-6 – "Trust in the Lord with all your heart and lean not on your own understanding; In all your ways acknowledge Him, And He will make your paths straight." (NASB)

Even though you don't always, unconditionally trust others, you can no longer afford not to do so. If God always, unconditionally gives love to you despite your flaws, how can you then not give the same Godly love to others? You must learn to love just as God already loves each and everyone of us. You are called upon to emulate God's love for you by also unconditionally giving love to others by always trusting them, no matter what.

Sadly, I can't think of another profession that goes against this foundation of Godly love and teaches you not to trust others more than being a police officer. From the very first days of training, you quickly learn not to trust others. It is repeatedly drilled into your way of thinking. It becomes an important part of your overall belief in officer safety and lies at the very core of how you're trained to perform your job.

Even though occasionally I was lucky enough to encounter a truly trustworthy person while on the job, I was constantly bombarded with the thought process that I couldn't afford to trust anyone who

The Greatest Gift Ever

didn't come from within that "thin blue line." I soon developed the belief that not only my life but also the lives of my fellow officers depended upon the existence of a negative atmosphere that bred a constant lack of trust towards anyone or anything outside our thin blue line.

Although that mindset served a purpose in keeping me sharp and focused while working, it soon developed into a separate issue that is hard for me to admit today. I discovered the hard way that I kept that lack of trust mindset going even when I wasn't working. I couldn't turn it off, and it almost became too much for me to bear. I finally realized there was a problem after I stopped trusting everyone, including members of my own family. To say that was a sobering reality would definitely be an understatement.

No one except other cops seemed to understand what I was going through at the time. And as if that wasn't enough to deal with, I also started turning into a control freak. I fooled myself into believing that, somehow, I was in control of my life, not God. I'm sure you've already figured out how well that one worked out for me. But the control issues didn't stop there. Oh no. I had the nerve to also try to control my family and all the relationships that existed outside of our family. Needless to say, my lack of trust didn't reflect to anyone that I had any Godly love burning inside of me.

Isaiah 26:3-4 – "You will keep in perfect peace all who trust in you, all whose thoughts are fixed on you! Trust in the Lord always, for the Lord God is the eternal Rock." (NLT)

Romans 15:13 – "I pray that God, the source of hope, will fill you completely with joy and peace because you trust in him. Then you will overflow with confident hope through the power of the Holy Spirit." (NLT)

Love Always Hopes

Having hope means you believe, trust, or expect everything to eventually turn out for the best. Lump in "always," and you can clearly see that having hope means to forever believe or forever trust in God's love, no matter what. Is Godly love even possible without hope? I doubt it. I can't speak for everyone else, but for me hope is what helped me go through many of the hard times I have experienced in life. I believe that hope is such a crucial aspect of God's whole love blueprint, because without it, how could you ever, forever believe that your future will turn out brighter?

We all know what usually happens when we lose hope. Been there, done that. When it's gone, it's gone. That's usually when we decide to give up and call it quits. Standing fast and holding firmly onto hope is how you keep from ever losing it. You should always keep your eyes on the prize.

If we are always, unconditionally giving love to others, is it even possible for us to lose hope in the first place? If you answered yes, I believe you're looking at the situation through your human eyes. I know the same picture wouldn't even exist if we were looking at this from God's perspective. After all, does God ever lose hope in us? If that were true, I don't think God would have ever loved us so much that He would have given His son so that we would have eternal life and be called children of God. I believe that calls for a resounding "Amen!"

In Groeschel's book, *From This Day Forward: Five Commitments to Fail-Proof Your Marriage*, the last commitment required of married couples is to never give up and to never quit, no matter what. You are in it to win it, so to speak. When we marry, we commit to never losing hope in our husband or wife. That being said, taking this commitment even further also means there is no place for divorce in your marriage, either. You never feel like getting divorced, you never think about divorce, and you never say the word divorce. You must commit to removing the word divorce from your vocabulary from the very beginning of your marriage. "Love Always Hopes" means you take your marriage as it was meant to be, a life-long commitment between the two of you and God. In essence, you will always, unconditionally give love to your husband or wife by never losing hope in them or your marriage, no matter what.

That is what makes this whole Godly love blueprint so amazing. God gave us each a puzzle piece to help us build a more solid Christian foundation, thus enabling us to love others as God loves us. One piece can't exist without the other, and each piece builds upon the others to reveal God's perfect plan for Godly love that all His children are called upon to follow and fulfill.

Godly love doesn't exist without hope, and neither can any of your relationships, especially your marriage. To love someone means to never lose hope in them or the relationship. It is critical that you change your thought process and begin to always, unconditionally give love to others by never losing hope in them, no matter what. Once you do, you will see a change in yourself, the other person, and the relationship.

Psalm 25:5 – "Lead me by your truth and teach me, for you are the God who saves me. All day long I put my hope in you." (NLT)

Psalm 31:24 – "Be strong and take heart, all you who hope in the Lord." (NIV)

Psalm 33:22 – "May your unfailing love be with us, Lord, even as we put our hope in You." (NIV)

Psalm 62:5 – "My soul, wait in silence for God only, For my hope is from Him." (NASB)

Psalm 71:14 – "As for me, I will always have hope; I will praise you more and more." (NIV)

Psalm 119:114 – "You are my refuge and my shield; your word is my source of hope." (NLT)

If you find yourself struggling with this concept, don't beat yourself up about it. Believe me when I tell you that, regardless of what has happened previously, if you strive to love as God loves, then your marriage can become what God intended it to be all along. Don't ever lose hope, and don't ever quit, no matter what.

I only know this because it almost happened to Lori and me. We almost gave up hope in our own marriage. Remember in the very beginning I revealed I had to write Lori an apology letter? Not too long ago, we were on the path of ending our marriage. The sad thing was we weren't even aware of it until it was almost too late. I can't speak for Lori, but my fault lay in the simple fact that I wasn't always, unconditionally giving love to her.

I can give you many excuses as to why that was the case but, ultimately, it doesn't even really matter. What matters is that I wasn't doing my part. I wasn't allowing God's love for me to change me into who God had called me to be. For some reason I was holding something back. I wasn't being a proper

The Greatest Gift Ever

Christian, husband, or father and, as such, it negatively impacted my relationship with God, Lori, Sarah, and Robyn.

Oh, I talked the talk, but those closest to me knew I wasn't walking the walk. On the outside I looked like I had it all together, but on the inside I was a complete mess. I struggled daily with sin. I allowed my pride and my illusion of being in control of my life to constantly cloud my better judgment. I made poor decisions almost daily. I wasn't being the child of God I was supposed to be. Nothing seemed to make me happy, and I blamed everyone else, including God, when the fault lay with me alone.

Here's the kicker: I had everything I needed to turn around and walk in the other direction back towards God, but I chose not to for the longest time. Looking back on it now, I know one of my biggest challenges was my inability to fully surrender to God. I don't know why I struggled with that. I guess I tried to trick myself into believing that I would somehow be better off if I didn't give all of me to Him. Those of you who have been there can relate. For those who can't relate, I hope you've done a much better job than I did.

Thankfully, God never gave up on me. He continued to always, unconditionally give His love to me even during my darkest hours. At first His love was in the form of what I like to refer to today as "the gentle knock at my door." God continued to knock gently at my door for the longest time. For whatever reason, I never wanted to answer my door. I heard the knocking, and I even knew God was knocking. I thought ignoring Him would eventually make it all go away. This is when it's very appropriate to say something like, "Craig, you're an idiot," and I would totally agree. But wait, it gets better.

Over the years God's knock became a little more frequent and even got louder as I continued to try to ignore it. God's love kept on coming, until finally one day, don't ask me how because I don't remember, I found myself on my hands and knees praying to God like I had never prayed before. I was crying uncontrollably and shaking from head to toe like a big ole baby. There I was, the big, bad cop unable to control any of my emotions or what was happening. Before I knew it, I was repenting all my sins and was finally releasing all the negative things that had built up inside me through the years. The whole experience felt almost as wonderful as the day I was saved. For the first time in a long time, I was finally standing again on God's solid, holy ground. It wasn't an easy experience, but that merciful "from God ah ha" moment helped me to put my life back on track and begin my whole Godly love transformation.

Romans 5:5 – "And this hope will not lead to disappointment. For we know how dearly God loves us, because he has given us the Holy Spirit to fill our hearts with his love." (NLT)

Colossians 1:5 – "We thank God for the hope that is being kept for you in heaven. You first heard about this hope through the Good News which is the Word of Truth." (NLV)

1 Peter 1:3 – "Blessed be the God and Father of our Lord Jesus Christ, who according to His great mercy has caused us to be born again to a living hope through the resurrection of Jesus Christ from the dead, …" (NASB)

Love Always Perseveres

To persevere means to have a steady persistence in a course of action, a purpose, especially in spite of difficulties, obstacles, or discouragement.

In theology, perseverance describes the continuance in a state of grace in the face of difficulties until the very end, which leads to eternal salvation. Some synonyms for perseverance are doggedness, steadfastness, persistence, and tenacity. Combine perseverance with "always," and Godly love, and then perseverance becomes *forever continuing in a course of action regardless of the obstacles, which will result in eternal salvation at the end.* Perseverance is a blessing from God that flourishes inside of you.

As with other aspects of God's whole love blueprint, perseverance is placed precisely where it's most appropriate – immediately following hope. In essence, to persevere in Godly love requires you to remain steadfast forever by choosing to always, unconditionally give love to others, no matter what. Just as with many of the other blueprint elements, to truly express Godly love you must understand that you are also called to persevere in your pursuit of applying God's love along your journey.

Unfortunately, there's a catch, as with most of the Godly love elements. Perseverance is the will you have inside that allows you to carry on despite those difficult situations or huge obstacles you encounter during your Christian journey. God gives you the strength you need to overcome each difficult situation, and your faith becomes stronger thanks to the perseverance indwelling inside of you. Each time you persevere through the storms in your life, the more successful your Christian walk eventually becomes.

Romans 5:1-4 – "Now that we have been made right with God by putting our trust in Him, we have peace with Him. It is because of what our Lord Jesus Christ did for us. By putting our trust in God, He has given us His loving-favor and has received us. We are happy for the hope we have of sharing the shining-greatness of God. We are glad for our troubles also. We know that troubles help us learn not to give up. When we have learned not to give up, it shows we have stood the test. When we have stood the test, it gives us hope." (NLV)

Romans 15:4 – "You see, everything written in the days of old was recorded to give us instructions *for living.* We find encouragement through the Scriptures and a call to perseverance that will produce hopeful living." (VOICE)

2 Corinthians 6:4 – "In everything we do, we show that we are true ministers of God. We patiently endure troubles and hardships and calamities of every kind." (NLT)

1 Timothy 6:11 – "But you, Timothy, are a man of God; so run from all these evil things. Pursue righteousness and a godly life, along with faith, love, perseverance, and gentleness." (NLT)

Hebrews 10:36 – "You need to persevere so that when you have done the will of God, you will receive what he has promised." (NIV)

James 1:12 – "Blessed is the one who perseveres under trial because, having stood the test, that person will receive the crown of life that the Lord has promised to those who love him." (NIV)

Revelation 3:10 – "Because you have obeyed my command to persevere, I will protect you from the great time of testing that will come upon the whole world to test those who belong to this world." (NLT)

Love Never Fails

Both the NASB and NLT Bibles use the word "fails" nine times; it's found 14 times in the NKJV Bible, NIV Bible, and NRSV Bible; and 16 times in the VOICE Bible *(biblegateway.com)*. To fail means many things but, in short, it could be defined as simply as not achieving a goal.

In the context of God's whole love blueprint, I believe God was referring to "fails" as something that is proven deficient or lacking; performed ineffectively or inadequately; proven insufficient in quantity or duration; given out; or made otherwise useless as a result of excessive strain (*thefreedictionary.com*). "Never" simply means "not ever." By combining those two words pertaining to Godly love, we now understand that "Love Never Fails" means that God's love transforms into not ever becoming inadequate or that it doesn't ever give out, no matter what difficulties are in your way. This last aspect of the blueprint reveals that Godly love lasts forever and doesn't ever end. I believe that is cause for another Amen! Wow!

In that sense, adding "Love Never Fails" as the last element in your new understanding of the Godly

Godly Love

love blueprint finally completes the puzzle. It provides all the motivation you need to follow each step of God's whole love blueprint; with it, you'll never fail because you're armed with a better understanding on how to properly imitate Godly love. Your desire to succeed will never be broken, crushed, or give out over time. You will never fail. Your new Godly love understanding will be so solid and so strong that nothing will ever keep you from achieving your goal of always, unconditionally giving love to others, no matter what. That is truly cause for celebration, and it's all because you choose to love others as your God already loves you. Wasn't that a message worth waiting for? Go ahead, you can say it–Amen!

Psalm 73:26 – "My flesh and my heart may fail, but God is the strength of my heart and my portion forever." (NIV)

Psalm 89:28 – "I will maintain my love to him forever, and my covenant with him will never fail." (NIV)

1 Corinthians 13:8 – "Love never fails. But where there are prophecies, they will cease; where there

The Greatest Gift Ever

are tongues, they will be stilled; where there is knowledge, it will pass away." (NIV)

A NEW PERSPECTIVE

I don't know about you, but after unpacking each element of God's love blueprint, I understood once and for all what Godly love was from His perspective. Yes, the light bulb finally went off. I hope you, too, are no longer in the dark. It was a huge burden lifted off my shoulders. I can no longer view love through my human eyes by attaching my emotions and feelings to the mix. I'm called, instead, to see Godly love through His eyes. I get very excited when I think of all the wonderful possibilities that exist for me when it comes to how I will choose to love going forward, as I understand now how much God already loves me.

Lori and I attend a local Christian church in central Pennsylvania. Our church's mission statement is simply to love God, love God's people, and love

God's world. Amazing how that mission statement is such a great reflection of what it truly means to imitate Godly love.

During a recent service, one of our members spoke about 1 Corinthians 13:1-8, when he gave the meditation message for communion. What caught my attention the most was when he decided to replace love with God in those verses. With your new understanding of God's whole love blueprint, see how those verses appear through your Godly love eyes now:

1 Corinthians 13:1-8 – If I speak in the tongues of men or of angels, but do not have **God**, I am only a resounding gong or a clanging cymbal. If I have the gift of prophecy and can fathom all mysteries and all knowledge, and if I have a faith that can move mountains, but do not have **God**, I am nothing. If I give all I possess to the poor and give over my body to hardship that I may boast, but do not have **God**, I gain nothing. **God** is patient, **God** is kind. **God** does not envy, **God** does not boast, **God** is not proud. **God** does not dishonor others, **God** is not self-seeking, **God** is not easily angered, **God** keeps no record of wrongs. **God** does not delight in

A New Perspective

evil but rejoices with the truth. ***God*** always protects, ***God*** always trusts, ***God*** always hopes, ***God*** always perseveres. ***God*** never fails.

If your reaction was anything like mine, it not only was a resounding "wow," but it also came with a huge side of "ah ha." Sadly, I recall how foreign that whole concept used to be to me. Thankfully, how uncomplicated it appears to me now. God placed all of His simple-to–follow instructions within His whole love blueprint from the very beginning. They have always been there as a guide for all of us to follow, but it took until very recently before I finally understood what it all really meant. I thank God for each and every one of His "from God ah ha" moments.

As the speaker continued in his meditation message, he made it all even more challenging by having us place our name in place of God's within the following Bible verses:

1 Corinthians 13:4-8 – ***Craig*** is patient, ***Craig*** is kind. ***Craig*** does not envy, ***Craig*** does not boast, ***Craig*** is not proud. ***Craig*** does not dishonor others, ***Craig*** is not self-seeking, ***Craig*** is not easily angered, ***Craig*** keeps no record of wrongs. ***Craig*** does not delight in evil but rejoices with the truth. ***Craig*** always protects, ***Craig*** always trusts, ***Craig*** always hopes, ***Craig*** always perseveres. ***Craig*** never fails.

Wow is right! I wish I could say that was all true. It was very humbling, to say the least, to read those verses in that fashion. I realized then that I still have a long way to go before I can confidently place my name in those verses. I know I'm not perfect, and there will be many days ahead when I'll struggle to successfully read those same verses after placing my name within them. But I'm encouraged and excited knowing that I now have the ability to finally begin to always, unconditionally give love to others, no matter what, because God already loves me that much. All I have to do is try and, ultimately, that is all we should ever strive for in the first place. I know I have already won by choosing to begin my transformation. The most difficult challenge was deciding to take that first step. It should be all down hill now, right?

Exodus 15:13 – "In your unfailing love you will lead the people you have redeemed. In your strength you will guide them to your holy dwelling." (NIV)

Psalm 26:3 – "Your unfailing love is always before me; I have journeyed down Your *path of truth*." (VOICE)

Psalm 31:16 – "Let your face shine on your servant; save me in your unfailing love." (NIV)

Psalm 85:7 – "O Eternal One, show us Your unfailing love; give us *what we truly need*: Your salvation." (VOICE)

Psalm 117:2 – "For His unfailing love is great, and it is *intended* for us, and His faithfulness *to His promises* knows no end. Praise the Eternal!" (VOICE)

Psalm 143:8 – "Cause me to hear thy lovingkindness in the morning; For in thee do I trust: Cause me to know the way wherein I should walk; For I lift up my soul unto thee." (ASV)

Romans 8:35 – "Who shall separate us from the love of Christ? *Shall* tribulation, or distress, or persecution, or famine, or nakedness, or peril, or sword?" (NKJV)

Achieving Godly Love

Start at the bottom and build your new Godly love foundation upwards. You'll get to the top eventually. Once you start building, don't ever give up. You have everything you need to begin. Just decide to take that first step today, and keep your eyes on the prize.

You must never fail
You must always hope; *you* must always persevere
You must always protect; *you* must always trust
You must not rejoice in evil; *you* must rejoice in the truth
You must not be easily angered; *you* must not keep records of wrongs
You must not be self-seeking; *you* must not dishonor others
You must not be proud; *you* must not boast
You must not envy
You must be kind
You must be patient

As I was doing some additional studying about the 16 aspects that comprise God's love blueprint, another "from God" moment came into my head. I never realized it until God revealed it to me. I was a little disappointed in myself that it had remained hidden from my eyes before that "ah ha" moment. If you number each aspect/element, starting with patient (#1) and ending with fails (#16), all the odd ones are stored inside of us, whereas all the even ones flow out of us.

Godly love begins with an inward ability and is then immediately followed up by an outward ability. Dissecting the very first two gives us a much clearer picture of how God's love blueprint actually works. God wants you to be transformed by first learning the ability to be patient, which Godly love has placed within you. After you learn patience, God's love further transforms you by the kindness that subsequently pours out of you.

The same becomes true for the next two abilities and so forth. Godly love builds upon the last ability you learned, beginning with an inward transformation that's followed next by an outward one. You continue along your journey of better comprehending God's love by learning each new ability, one after the other. It might seem a little easier to understand by looking at it from this perspective:

> Being Patient (in) > Being Kind (out)
> Do Not Envy (in) > Do Not Boast (out)
> Do Not Be Proud (in) > Do Not Dishonor (out)
> Not Self-seeking (in) > Not Easily Angered (out)
> No Record of Wrongs (in) > Do Not Delight in Evil (out)
> Delights in the Truth (in) > Always Protects (out)
> Always Trusts (in) > Always Hopes (out)
> Always Perseveres (in) > Never Fails (out)

Hopefully, looking at Godly love from another new perspective will provide you all the motivation you need to begin the transformation. It's crucial that you learn to always, unconditionally give love to others, no matter what. Keep your eyes on the prize. Never stop. Never quit.

1 Corinthians 2:9 – "The Holy Writings say, 'No eyes have ever seen or no ear has ever heard or no mind has ever thought of the wonderful things God has made ready for those who love Him.' " (NLV)

THE HEART OF THE MATTER

I find all of this to be very interesting. Who ever imagined that the key to our success here on earth was learning what the greatest gift ever was? The concept sounds so easy and so simple, right? This should be something we are all capable of not only comprehending but also fulfilling. Yet if you're like me, most of us will struggle with this whole concept the majority of our time here on earth. Don't think for an instant that just because you're a child of God that you automatically get it, either. Why? In the end, we're all still human. Our first instinct is to think and react as humans. This goes back to the point that we mess up how and why we love. We allow our emotions and feelings to guide our love instead of unconditionally giving love to.

The Greatest Gift Ever

So where do we begin? Let's take a little journey together to figure this one out. Imagine a place where it's dark, cold, damp and dreary. It's a scary place. It's a cloudy, foggy place. You can't seem to see more than just a few inches in any direction. You can hear so many sounds going on all around you, but you can't make sense of any of them. Sometimes it sounds like someone is crying. Other times you can hear someone shouting. Every now and then you can hear yelling and screaming, but you don't know where it is coming from.

It's all around you. It's a place where all your worst fears exist. It's a place of broken pieces and shattered dreams. A place where your worst nightmares came true, and every bad situation you ever experienced haunts you. We never want to be in this place, and yet we spend the majority of our lives constantly running to and from it. Try as we may, it always seems to catch up to us. No matter what we do, it's never far from our thoughts.

We can try to deny it, but in the end we know it's there. It's always been there. We wish it were only a dream. Unfortunately, this place does exist. We've been there so many times during our lives. Can you picture such a place? Have you ever been to such a place? I know I have. So have you guessed it yet? Where does this awful, horrible place exist? Would you be surprised to learn that it's our very own heart?

Why would our heart ever be such a place, you ask? Because how we learn and choose to love comes from our hearts. Learning how to love properly means you have to change your heart. Your transformation must begin there.

Psalm 19:14 – "Let the words of my mouth and the thoughts of my heart be pleasing in Your eyes, O Lord, my Rock and the One Who saves me." (NLV)

Psalm 119:10 – "With all my heart I have sought You; Do not let me wander from Your commandments." (NASB)

Psalm 139:23-24 – "Search me, God, and know my heart; test me and know my anxious thoughts. See if there is any offensive way in me, and lead me in the way everlasting." (NIV)

Proverbs 4:23 – "Guard your heart above all else, for it determines the course of your life." (NLT)

Proverbs 15:13 – "A glad heart makes a happy face, but when the heart is sad, the spirit is broken." (NLV)

Luke 16:15 – "He said to them, You are the ones who justify yourselves in the eyes of others, but God knows your hearts. What people value highly is detestable in God's sight." (NIV)

Hebrews 4:12 – "For the word of God is alive and active. Sharper than any double-edged sword, it penetrates even to dividing soul and spirit, joints and marrow; it judges the thoughts and attitudes of the heart." (NIV)

It simply comes down to the heart of the matter. To begin your transformation into maturing, changing, and becoming more like Jesus Christ, you must first begin that transformation within your heart. I can't stress this enough: you will never truly experience the type of relationship God wants with each and every one of His children until you choose to change your heart. It isn't easy, but it's crucial that you begin to do so. Without this change, living in harmony with God will always be extremely difficult, if not next to impossible, for you to achieve.

Just how crucial is changing your heart to God's whole love blueprint? So important that the word "heart" is used 926 times in the NKJV Bible, 902 times in the NLV Bible, 896 times in the ASV Bible, 886 times in the NRSV Bible, 805 times in the NASB, 762 times in the VOICE Bible, 725 times in the NIV Bible, and 573 times in the NLT Bible (*biblegateway. com*). Get the picture yet? For those of you who struggle with this heart concept, trust me, I've been where you are. For those who've already crossed that goal line, I congratulate you, because you're a lot farther along in your transformation than most.

Psalm 9:1 – "I will give thanks to the LORD with my whole heart; I will tell of all your wonderful deeds." (NRSV)

Psalm 10:17 – "O Lord, You have heard the prayers of those who have no pride. You will give strength to their heart, and You will listen to them." (NLV)

Proverbs 23:26 – "Give me your heart, my son. Let your eyes find joy in my ways." (NLV)

The Greatest Gift Ever

Matthew 5:8 – "Blessed are the pure in heart, for they will see God." (NIV)

2 John 1:6 – "Love means that we should live by obeying His Word. From the beginning He has said in His Word that our hearts should be full of love." (NLV)

MY JOURNEY

To those who still feel they're struggling, let me share another part of my journey with you in hopes that it will inspire you to realize that anyone can choose to change their hearts. I worked in the law enforcement field for most of my life. I also spent over 14 years serving my country. First I enlisted in the US Navy, and then I transferred into the US Army. While in the US Army, I served for over 12 years as a Special Agent in both Counterintelligence and with the Criminal Investigation Command (CID). Of the two, being a CID Agent was definitely the hardest. More on that point a little later.

Even though I considered myself a Christian during my time in the military, I definitely wasn't walking the walk or talking the talk. I was silent and kept my faith hidden. I didn't share with anyone,

The Greatest Gift Ever

including Lori, what I believed. Embarrassing as it was, I'm sure you would be hard pressed to find anyone I served with who would state that they knew I was a Christian or that my actions reflected that God was alive inside of me. I hope that change became more noticeable towards the end of my career.

One of the hardest experiences I've ever gone through was when my father died of cancer at the young age of 48, when I was 21. Until his death, I had never experienced the loss of a loved one first hand. My father's death was very hard for me for several reasons, the primary one being that my relationship with God barely existed. I wasn't growing in or with Him. Lori and I didn't attend church, and I wasn't leading my family as a Christian husband should. Some of my flaws were due to the fact that after being saved, I had never learned how to grow in my relationship with God. To be honest, I didn't even know then who I was in God or who my God truly was.

My overall attitude towards God during that time was similar to my relationship with my earthly father. The few times I did go to church, the majority of sermons I remembered hearing only seemed to reflect an angry, jealous, and vengeful God. I felt a sense

My Journey

of hopelessness, that I was a reflection of God's people in the Old Testament. Despite God's efforts, I kept messing up my relationship with Him by continuing to violate His commandments.

I also had a flawed foundation when it came to prayer. I had never learned the reasons for prayer and why praying was so important for my continued growth. I should have been praying for things like wisdom, faith, and guidance, but I found myself instead praying for things that were motivated by my own selfish wants and needs. After those prayers always seemed to go unanswered, I began to think I wasn't worthy. I felt God was angry with me. I hadn't changed into the Christian I was supposed to be, because I couldn't stop sinning. As a result I started questioning and doubting my salvation. I just seemed incapable of making things right with God. My faith then became stagnant, and I stopped going to church. Although I maintained my belief in God, I wasn't doing anything proactive to help that faith grow.

Psalm 119:11 – "I have hidden your word in my heart that I might not sin against you." (NIV)

The Greatest Gift Ever

Another reason my dad's death was difficult for me was because I wasn't being the Christian husband I was called to be at that time. Even though Lori and I had been saved and baptized before we met, I didn't place God at the center of our marriage because I didn't know how to. I wasn't leading us properly towards continued dependency and growth in God. God should have been in control of my marriage from the beginning, but I chose not to surrender. The path I chose for us wasn't immersed in God. I wasn't a reflection of Godly love in everything I did. I allowed my emotions and feelings to hinder my ability to always unconditionally give love to Lori.

Needless to say, when my dad died I didn't deal with it as a well as I could have if my faith had been stronger. Instead I became a very angry person. I was angry with myself, but I was probably angrier with God. I took that anger out on everyone, especially Lori. I know that my anger during this time also affected my relationship with our first-born daughter, Sarah.

Part of my anger stemmed from not taking advantage of the time I did have with my father to reconcile with him before he passed. Don't get me wrong, my father wasn't a bad father. But my relationship with him wasn't what it could have been. For many reasons, we seemed to clash all the time. I don't ever remember a time when he told me he loved me or that he was proud of me. I spent the majority of my young life trying to win his love, his approval, and to make him proud of me. Unfortunately, that same thought process transferred over to God. I thought I had to also win God's love and approval.

Before my dad died, there was a beautiful song out by Mike and the Mechanics called "The Living Years." The part of the song that struck deep into my heart was when Mike reminded us that he "wasn't there that morning when my father passed away" and that he "didn't get to tell him all the things" he "had to say." I made that my theme song and vowed that I would say all the things I needed to say to my father while he was still alive. I wanted to reconcile with him before it was too late. I wanted him to know I loved him and that he did his best to be a good father. I wanted him to know that I forgave him. I wanted each of us to let go of anything negative inside we were harboring towards each other. I also needed to hear him tell me I was forgiven for all my shortcomings. But more importantly, I needed to hear him tell me that he loved me and was proud of me.

During my father's battle with non-Hodgkin's Lymphoma, he never appeared to be that sick. I was in the US Navy at the time, and we were stationed in Norfolk, Virginia. Lori and I would come home frequently for visits. During those visits, my dad had lost some weight and his hair, but he still seemed to be okay. We were able to interact with him as if he really wasn't too sick with cancer after all. Even though my goal was to reconcile with him before it was too late, I took for granted there would always be a tomorrow based upon how his battle with cancer was unfolding. I felt the urge to reconcile with my dad grow stronger as time passed, but I didn't know how to begin. My list of excuses grew in my head as each visit passed without fulfilling my goal. About a year into his battle with cancer, it appeared as if he was going to make a full recovery. Little did I realize it at the time, but things were about to change.

Unfortunately, his battle with cancer did change. That change was very quick and quite unexpected. To make matters worse, it came shortly after I had transferred to the US Army, and we were now stationed even farther away in Alabama. On July 2, 1989. I got the call from my mom that I needed to come home right away. My father had undergone a radical treatment for his cancer, and his condition after this treatment became critical. I frantically worked out all the details and went on emergency leave later that day. Lori and I drove all night to get to my parent's house in Alexandria, Virginia. After we arrived, we went straight to the hospital. When I entered the room and saw my dad lying there, I couldn't believe my eyes. He didn't even look like my father. He had lost a lot of weight. He was very skinny and looked to me like he was a skeleton. I barely recognized him. To make matters worse, he was incoherent and couldn't speak. He was also heavily medicated. When he looked at me, I felt he didn't even recognize me. I lost it. For one of the few moments in my life, I began to cry uncontrollably. I had never seen my dad like this. For the first time since his battle with cancer began, he actually looked like he was sick.

That moment should have been my clue that my next step was to immediately reconcile with him, but I didn't. To this day I still don't know why I didn't. After a few hours of being in the room with my parents,

The Greatest Gift Ever

Lori and I left to get some rest at their house, as my mom was staying at the hospital taking care of my dad. The next morning we got up early and returned to the hospital to visit them. Again, I should have taken advantage of this time to reconcile, but I didn't.

As that day wore on, my father began to show significant improvements in his condition. The doctors were optimistic and felt that he might even recover. When we left later in the day, I went to say goodbye to him. As I was talking to him in his ear saying goodbye, he turned towards me and kissed my cheek. He still couldn't talk. At first I was shocked, because I don't ever remember my father kissing me before. That should have been the final clue I needed to reconcile with him right there and then. For whatever reason, I again chose not to. I would soon discover that I would regret that decision for years to come.

Later that night I had fallen asleep on the couch while watching television. I woke up as my mom and uncle came through the front door. Without saying a word I could tell by the look on my mom's face that my dad had passed away. I remember waking Lori up to let her know my dad had died. She did her best to console me.

I don't know why, but for some reason I wanted to go to the hospital right away. I guess I wanted to go in a futile effort to somehow fix my earlier decision not to reconcile. I was sad and also became very angry. I didn't know it at the time, but that sadness and anger was going to consume me for a long time. I took my anger out on God and everyone else around me. I blamed God, but in reality it was my fault. I held onto it for many years to come, because I didn't know how to deal with it or how to let it go.

It took a long time to recover from that experience. There were more unnecessary arguments between Lori and me because of my anger than I care to admit or remember. We made numerous attempts to "fix" things through individual as well as couple's counseling sessions. Nothing seemed to work. I allowed my anger to drive such a wedge between God and me. Unfortunately, that wedge also affected my marriage and my children.

John 13:34 – "A new commandment I give to you, that you love one another, even as I have loved you, that you also love one another." (NASB)

John 16:33 – "I have told you these things, so that in Me you may have peace. In this world you will have trouble. But take heart! I have overcome the world." (NIV)

THE BEGINNING OF MY TRANSFORMATION

I didn't know it at the time, but several years later God was going to change my life completely around. At times I felt God allowed me to deal with my anger in my own way. I know it was always an illusion that I somehow was the one in control and not God. That illusion helped to serve God's purpose for some long overdue needed changes in my life. Thankfully, God was never too far away from me during all those rough times. Slowly but surely, God began to complete the work He began in me so many years earlier. At times my journey forward was going to be very difficult, but luckily it would all be worth it in the end.

This transformation began when I was stationed in South Korea for a one-year, unaccompanied tour without Lori and Sarah. It was a long and difficult tour without them. Although I missed them both very much, the time apart turned out to be just exactly what I needed to begin reflecting on my life. Through a variety of feelings of both emptiness and despair, I soon came to the realization of exactly how poorly I had treated them. This realization didn't happen overnight, but in time it allowed my heart to began to change.

After my tour in South Korea, I was then assigned to a three-year accompanied tour to of all places Hawaii. I know, you're thinking "really tough duty," huh? Shortly after our arrival in Hawaii, we welcomed our second daughter, Robyn. About a year and a half into this tour, an opportunity arose and I decided to change jobs. This is when I began the transfer from Counterintelligence into CID. I started working as an Intern Investigator for the local CID office while my application into CID was being processed. It was during my internship that I also decided to finally finish my college education and started attending a local university in Hawaii full time at night.

As part of my elective credits, I had to take a religion class. At first I wasn't happy at all about having

The Beginning of My Transformation

to take that class. After putting it off as long as possible, I settled on a class that taught an overview on the world's religions. That course reignited the fire I once had inside of me for God. Eventually, that spark helped begin my long journey back to God and paved the way for me to be where I am today.

In the spring of 1998, I graduated with a Bachelor's of Science Degree in Criminal Justice. In July of 1998, I graduated from CID school and was transferred to New Jersey, of all places. It was there that God chose again to rock my world.

Psalm 83:1 – "O God, do not remain quiet; Do not be silent and, O God, do not be still." (NASB)

Proverbs 9:9 – "Instruct the wise and they will be wiser still; teach the righteous and they will add to their learning." (NIV)

1 Corinthians 15:17 – "… and if Christ has not been raised, your faith is worthless; you are still in your sins." (NASB)

THE MEETING

Soon after our arrival in New Jersey, Lori and the girls began attending a local Christian church. Every Sunday morning before they left, Lori would ask me if I wanted to go with them. I refused each time — politely, probably mostly sarcastically or, even more so, angrily. I never really had a good excuse for not going with them other than I felt I was still angry with God. This went on for a few months, until one day I finally challenged Lori's request to go to church. I told her that if the church's pastor agreed to meet with me to answer some of my questions, then in return I would go to church with them. It's funny now but, at the time, the look on Lori's face reflected sheer terror.

Lori was a little skeptical, to say the least. Okay, probably more like a lot scared and skeptical. She bounced our conversation off of our next door neighbor, whose family also attended that church. Our neighbor took the ball and ran with it. She approached the church pastor and told him about my family's situation and my subsequent challenge. Surprisingly, he agreed to meet with me. Now picture this; Lori is attending a church that she's grown to enjoy. Along comes her husband with the biggest chip on his shoulder in the world against God, and he's now going to meet with the pastor to discuss his questions. Can you blame her for being very scared, worried, and skeptical? She gave me the date and time for the meeting a few days later and then proceeded to remind me how much she and the girls liked going to this church. She sternly warned me about the consequences I would face from her if I did anything to embarrass her or make them not welcome again at this church.

I don't remember the exact date, but I remember driving to the church and then waiting anxiously inside to meet with the pastor. Just a little backdrop, but my previous meetings with members of the clergy after my father's death had never helped to resolve my anger or answer my questions. Instead, they usually just fanned the flames, more often than not. My frustration during those meetings and the corresponding questions I raised almost every time resulted in being told that I was not allowed to question God or why He allowed certain things to happen. I was just supposed to accept these events, but questioning or even being angry with God was a sin. As you can imagine, these encounters didn't steer me back but instead kept me full speed ahead in the opposite direction. At least, so I thought.

So here I am at the church about to meet with the pastor. What happened next wasn't anything I was prepared for, based upon my previous clergy encounters. He was nothing like I expected. He wasn't much older than I was. In fact we were very close to the same age. I thought, wow, someone I might be able to relate to after all. Soon we began our conversation, and I asked him all the same questions I had asked others before. Things like, why did my dad have to die at such a young age? Why didn't I reconcile with my dad when I had the chance? Where was God in all of this? Why don't I feel worthy enough to accept my salvation? How do I begin a relationship with a God who never seems to answer any of my prayers? Why this and why that? The pastor allowed me to vent for a while. He

The Meeting

just sat there silently and listened. Then for the first time in my life I heard a clergyman say what I never expected to hear. He told me that he didn't have all the answers, and he couldn't tell me why certain things had transpired the way they did in my life. I sat there in disbelief. For the first time ever I asked a clergyman my questions, and I wasn't made to feel ashamed for asking them. From there our encounter developed into one of the most influential relationships ever in my life.

Lori nervously approached me when I returned home and inquired about the meeting. She really wanted to know if I had embarrassed her to the point that she had to find a new church and probably new neighbors, too. After we discussed the meeting, she was very relieved and also seemed a little encouraged about the outcome.

As part of the bargain I had made with Lori, I began going to church with my family again on a regular basis. The pastor took me under his wing and began to teach me not only how to have a relationship with God but also what that kind of relationship was supposed to look like. He even loaned me a few books to read, and we already know how much I like to read. But he was very patient with me and allowed me all the space I needed to finish those books in my time. He taught me how to spend time daily with God. His guidance and direction enabled me, for the first time in my life, to become closer to God.

The one book he asked me read that helped me the most in my quest to grow closer to God was Richard J. Foster's *Celebration of Discipline*. Within that book I learned about 10 different ways to spend time and grow closer to God. Meditation still remains my all-time favorite to this day. If it weren't for the pastor's guidance and teaching, I don't know when or if I would have ever decided to embark on my spiritual journey towards reconciling with God.

Psalm 18:46 – "The Lord lives, and blessed be my rock; And exalted be the God of my salvation, …" (NASB)

THE FINAL STRAW

Unfortunately for me, my new journey with God came at a huge price. To make a long story short, I soon began to realize more and more how ashamed I was of the person I had become. That shame echoed deep in my soul with all my failures as a Christian, husband, and father. I don't know why, but it brought me to the point in my life where I felt Lori, Sarah, and Robyn were better off without me. Something inside of me just wouldn't allow me to hold my head up high and be optimistic about the future. I had caused too much hurt and too much pain to my family. I didn't think they would ever forgive me for the past, when it actually boiled down to me not being able to forgive myself. I wasn't angry and disappointed with God. I was angry, disappointed with and ashamed of myself.

The Greatest Gift Ever

Without thinking about the ramifications and how it might affect my family, I mustered the courage to share with Lori how I felt. Talk about bad timing. At that time we were exact polar opposites and both moving forward in different directions. Lori was encouraged about our future and was relieved to see how I was slowly beginning to change for the better. We were going to church together as a family, and I was learning new things from the pastor. I, on the other hand, wasn't feeling good about myself. I couldn't get away from the fact that all of my past failures kept haunting me. I didn't understand how Lori could still love me after all I had put her through.

The next few days were filled with many emotions. Some were good, but most were bad ones. We decided to separate, and they would move back to Pennsylvania while I remained in New Jersey. I don't know if the girls, especially Sarah, understood any of what was happening. Luckily, Robyn was too young to understand it all.

As the date approached for their move back to Pennsylvania, I tried in vain to stop everything from happening. I didn't want to see them leave, but Lori stood her ground. We even tried a few counseling sessions with our pastor, but even that was futile.

I had hurt Lori again to the point that she felt convinced to go. She had lost faith in me, and I had hurt her for the last time. No more, she thought. Lori felt that if we didn't go through with this that I would only do this to her again somewhere down the road. Imagine hearing that coming from your wife? Sad thing is, she was probably right. After all, I already knew I hadn't been the best husband I should have been to her. The fact that she stood by my side through all my selfishness and anger during those many prior years says a lot about the wonderful Christian and wife she truly is.

After they left for Pennsylvania, I moved into an apartment complex on the base. I was continuing my time with the pastor and focused on growing closer with God. I didn't know it then, but I believe now that God orchestrated that time away from my family so He could continue the work He had begun in me. That isolation was what God felt I needed to begin my journey and move forward in my relationship with Him.

Needless to say, I had a lot of time to myself to reflect on my life up to that point. I soon began to come to grips with a lot of the mistakes and bad choices I had made along the way. I went through many highs and lows, but God was faithful during this time, as well. He kept me grounded, moving forward and focused on the reasons I needed to change. I would never become what He wanted me to be unless I changed.

My time with the pastor became increasingly rewarding. I still use today the lessons he taught me. I was reading many books that helped lay a more solid foundation for my faith, and he continued to teach me ways to spend time with God. It was during those times that I grew more than I ever had before. It was refreshing, to say the least.

In time, I believe Lori started to see some of the positive changes in me during our brief interactions when I was either returning the girls or she was dropping them off. Somewhere along the way, God intervened between us, and we slowly started to reconcile with each other.

After we decided to get back together, I had also made the tough decision to leave the military. I was very disappointed when I learned I was going to be transferred back to South Korea again for another unaccompanied one-year tour. I'd had enough and knew staying in wouldn't be beneficial to the direction I was headed in my life. More importantly, I

The Final Straw

didn't want anything to interfere with our reconciliation. I didn't see any benefit to being away from my family for another year. Ironically, when I finally did leave the military, it was exactly four weeks before 9/11. Was that just coincidence or was it another "from God" scenario? You can decide that one on your own.

Job 9:10 – "He does great things too marvelous to understand. He performs countless miracles." (NLT)

Daniel 4:2 – "I am pleased to be able to tell you about all the signs and miracles the Most High God has done for me." (VOICE)

Hebrews 2:4 – "And God confirmed the message by giving signs and wonders and various miracles and gifts of the Holy Spirit whenever he chose." (NLT)

OUR RENEWAL

Amazingly, God wasn't done working within Lori and me just yet. One of the best "from God" moments that came out of this whole unfortunate situation was our decision to get baptized together and renew our marriage vows. We couldn't think of a better person or a better place than with the pastor of that Christian church in New Jersey.

Even more amazing was our decision to write our own renewal vows. At the time it seemed like a very good idea. A public confession from me to Lori through the reciting of God-inspired words would be just the perfect setting we needed to continue along in our reconciliation. If you are thinking there was a catch, you are right.

I spent a lot of time rehearsing the vows I had written. I felt very confident that I almost had them all memorized. I thought the whole event was going to be easy p'easy. I felt that way just prior to the start of our ceremony. Right before we began, I suddenly became overfilled with emotion.

Unbeknownst to me at the time, but all of those deep, hidden, pent-up emotions were about to release "things" that I had buried deep down inside of me. They just started overtaking me. It was like wave after wave crashing against the shore. I soon started to cry. When it came time for me to read my vows, I had a very hard time reading them out loud at all. It was truly a very humbling experience for me, because I was reminded of all the wrongs I had done to Lori and the girls up until that point. I felt relieved but also simultaneously ashamed of the person I once was. I began crying uncontrollably. It wouldn't stop, and I couldn't turn it off. I couldn't even look at any of our family or friends who were gathered in the audience. I was too embarrassed and ashamed of what I used to be. I don't know how, but somehow I managed to finish reading those vows, all the while bawling like a baby.

That day began a new chapter in our lives. God was still working inside of me, and I had a new sense of faith I'd never known before. Although I knew I still had a long journey ahead, I was hopeful I was finally headed down the right path. Although this song hadn't been released yet before our renewal ceremony, I can't miss the opportunity to mention how appropriately Josh Wilson's song, "That Was Then, This Is Now," applies to this whole particular situation. Lori and I, through our renewal ceremony, had made the decision to leave our past in the past. We accepted the fact that going forward we were no longer the same two people we once used to be and that, with God's help, our marriage could become whatever we chose it to be.

Romans 12:2 – "Don't copy the behavior and customs of this world, but let God transform you into a new person by changing the way you think. Then you will learn to know God's will for you, which is good and pleasing and perfect." (NLT)

Ephesians 2:1-10 – "As for you, *don't you remember how you used to just exist? Corpses,* dead *in life,* buried by transgressions, wandering the course of this *perverse* world. *You were the offspring* of the prince of the power of air—*oh, how he owned you,* just as he still controls those living in disobedience. *I'm not talking about the outsiders alone;* we were all guilty of falling headlong for the persuasive passions of this world; we all have had our fill of indulging the flesh and mind, *obeying impulses to follow perverse thoughts motivated by dark powers.* As a result, our natural inclinations led us to be children of wrath, just like the rest of humankind. But God, with the *unfathomable* richness of His love and mercy focused on us, united us with the Anointed One and infused our lifeless souls with life—even though we were buried under mountains of sin—and saved us by His grace. He raised us up with Him and seated us in the heavenly realms with *our beloved* Jesus the Anointed, *the Liberating King. He did this for a reason:* so that for all eternity we will stand as a living testimony to the incredible riches of His grace and kindness that He freely gives to us by uniting us with Jesus the Anointed. For it's by God's grace that you have been saved. You receive it through faith. It was not *our plan or* our effort. It is God's gift, *pure and simple.* You didn't earn it, *not one of us did*, so don't go around bragging *that you must have done something amazing.* For we are the product of His hand, *heaven's poetry etched on lives,* created in the Anointed, Jesus, to accomplish the good works God arranged long ago." (VOICE)

THE END RESULT

In time that pastor became one of my closest friends, and we still keep in touch today. Even though we don't get to see much of each other in person anymore, we still have an occasional telephone conversation to catch up and share our journeys with one another. His friendship and teachings helped pave the way for me to return to my faith. I don't know where I would be today if he hadn't agreed to meet with a total stranger with a huge chip on his shoulder who was searching for some answers to many burning questions. I have no doubt that everything I experienced with him was definitely a "from God" thing. Even more encouraging for me was when I was able to realize that my meeting and subsequent relationship with him were answers to

The End Result

prayers I had made so many years ago. Crazy I know, but oh, so true.

Okay, so now you have my story on why I consider that learning how to always unconditionally give love to others is definitely "the heart of the matter." As I've shared, there's no way you'll begin to transform yourself into always, unconditionally giving love to others unless your heart is in the right place. It would have been impossible for me to attempt to love as God loves during all of those times in my life when my heart wasn't ready or open because it was filled with anger, hurt, sadness, and regret.

2 Corinthians 5:14-15 – "For the love of Christ controls us, having concluded this, that one died for all, there all died; and He died for all, so that they who love might no longer live for themselves, but for Him who died and rose again on their behalf." (NASB)

SEEING THINGS DIFFERENTLY

Changing your "***heart***" is the key to beginning your transformation. I believe beyond a doubt that in order for us to transform and become more like Christ, we must begin with what is in our hearts. Our very salvation and our fulfillment of our time here on earth depend upon it. It is the main hurdle we all must overcome to live in harmony with God. It will allow us to move closer and closer each day to becoming all that God created us to be.

Deuteronomy 30:16 – "in that I command you today to love the Lord your God, to walk in His ways and to keep His commandments and His statues and His judgments, that you may live and multiply, and that the Lord your God may bless you in the land where you are entering to possess it." (NASB)

Colossians 1:10 – "May their lives be a credit to You, Lord; and *what's more*, may they continue to delight You by doing every good work and growing in the true knowledge that comes from being close to You." (VOICE)

As I discussed earlier, my career in law enforcement had many rewards and challenges. Although I would gladly choose that profession if I had to do it all over again, my only wish would be to have a better understanding of what Godly love was when I started.

No one knows what it's like to be a police officer or an investigator until you have walked in those very same shoes. It is its own little world with its own unique group of people and its own series of experiences. If you aren't in that world or part of that group, then you're an outsider and, unfortunately, as we discussed earlier, you quickly learn not to trust outsiders.

Not to mention the fact that, in that line of work, you don't usually encounter very many good, law

The Greatest Gift Ever

abiding, religious minded people. Day after day, hour after hour, shift after shift, you normally only come across the worst society has to offer. Unless you keep the right perspective and stay focused, it's very easy to feel overwhelmed and to become consumed by all of that darkness you encounter, while constantly longing for that Godly love you feel you never see anymore.

If you aren't careful, in time you'll find yourself becoming cold, emotionless, and trying to wall yourself off from the rest of the world simply to protect yourself and your family. The enemy becomes everyone who isn't in your line of work, because no one else seems to understand all the different things you're going through. You're rarely thanked for what you do and are subjected to constant "Monday Morning Quarterbacking" for the split second decisions you made in order to survive and live to fight another day.

To make matters even worse, it wasn't until I was already several years into my law enforcement career before I realized all the progress I'd made before with God and my faith was going right out the window. I never saw it coming, but luckily I realized what was happening before it was too late.

Seeing Things Differently

If all those things weren't bad enough, you end up seeing things that most people never see. You experience things that no one should ever have to experience during their lifetime. Like how a mother could kick her four-year-old baby girl so hard that she ends up dying from that kick, all because she'd tipped over a basket of laundry that the mother had just folded. Then comes the hard part. As part of your job, you have to processes that baby girl's lifeless body for evidence. If that weren't enough, next comes the unfortunate gruesome experience of having to attend that little baby's autopsy. You watch as the coroner methodically combs her body in an attempt to determine the exact cause of her death. Then her body reveals where her mother kicked her. You witness first hand the effects of how blunt force trauma can break apart a little baby's abdomen. During this whole time, you're trying not to picture your own baby girl lying there in her place, and all the while you're also trying to understand why this little baby had to suffer such a painful, useless death.

An even more traumatic experience is being the first one to arrive on the scene where a husband has just shot his wife. From a distance you see her body lying halfway dressed in the street. As you approach,

The Greatest Gift Ever

you can hear her moaning because she can't speak. The moaning isn't unusual. You've heard it before, and it reminds you of the moaning someone does when they're in a lot of pain. You finally get close enough and can see that there's what appears to be a gunshot wound to her head. You notice that there's a large amount of blood gushing out of her body and pooling on the ground behind her. Based on her wounds, you know there's nothing you can do to save her life. She's dying right there in front of you. So you kneel down next to her, and taking her hand in yours, you hear and then slowly watch her die a painful, agonizing death. With her hand in yours, you don't utter a word, but somehow try to provide her with the comfort that she isn't dying alone.

Or what about the experience of arriving to process a scene where a human being shot another human being over some sort of turf battle? Blood and shell casings riddle the scene, then loved ones start arriving to the area. You see and hear people screaming and crying uncontrollably because someone just shot their loved one. They turn to you and shout "Why?" as if anything you could possibly say at that very moment would help them to understand the whole situation.

Seeing Things Differently

Still other memorable experiences involve having to inform a mother and father that their daughter had passed away after being involved in a vehicle accident. You witness events unfolding in real time, like seeing the tragic results after a husband returns home drunk and then proceeds to beat up his family.

Then, there are those many priceless encounters with people who call you every nasty, vulgar name in the book, including that you're a racist, all because you pulled them over after they decided to run a red light or failed to stop for a stop sign. Still nothing compares to the experience of being shot at, spit on, slapped, scratched, hit, kicked, punched, and even threatened, because you're dealing with another human being who is "high" on something other than life. Nope, being a cop is great. You get to experience all of those situations and many more.

Jeremiah 17:10 – "But I, the Lord, search all hearts and examine secret motives. I give all people their due rewards, according to what their actions deserve." (NLT)

Hebrews 2:1-3 – "That is why we ought to pay even closer attention to the voice that has been speaking so that we will never drift away from it. For if the words *of instruction and inspiration* brought by heaven's messengers were valid, and *if we live in a universe where* sin and disobedience receive their just rewards, then how will we escape *destruction* if we ignore this great salvation? We heard it first from our Lord Jesus, then from those who passed on His teaching." (VOICE)

STAYING FOCUSED

As I mentioned earlier, even though I started to become closer to God and my faith strengthened before embarking on my second career as a police officer, I still almost lost everything. Once I became aware of what was happening, I knew I had to make a change.

Thanks to another "from God ah ha moment," I knew I was changing, and not in a positive way. I realized, I needed to find someone I could talk to. Luckily my search lead me to a Christian counselor. With her help, I was able to put my life back into perspective, and get back on track. She had me go through several counseling sessions with other patients, focusing our time on Neil T. Anderson's book *Victory Over the Darkness: Realize the Power of Your Identity in Christ*. Reading that book and

The Greatest Gift Ever

completing the accompanying study guide was a total game changer for me. For the first time in my life I finally understood not only who God was but also who I was in Christ. Yes, my friend, another light bulb in my head finally turned on.

I was changed forever with a brand new, more solid faith foundation. I was on fire for God, and my faith was renewed like never before. I still don't know how, but shortly after completing my counseling, I found myself in one of our church pastor's offices begging him to allow me to hold a Bible study focusing on Anderson's book. I felt called to teach others about the truths contained within that book. Anderson's book subsequently became what I now jokingly refer to as Christianity 101 or, even better, Christianity for Dummies.

I finally realized and accepted that I was a child of God and believed that I deserved all the benefits that came as a result of membership in His family. I was even able to dump some more baggage that had been weighing me down for so many years. The whole experience was truly amazing and another example of a "from God ah ha" moment.

The best part was that for the first time ever, I held my own Bible study of that book. Class participants consisted not only of Lori but also of Sarah and her husband, along with other family members and friends. What a blessing it was to watch my loved ones and friends transform during our study and time together.

1 Peter 4:2-4 – "... so that you may live the rest of your life on earth *controlled* not by earthly desires but by the will of God. You have already wasted enough time living like those outsiders in the society around you: losing yourselves in sex, in addictions and desires, in drinking and lawless idolatry, in *giving your time and* allegiance to things that are not godly. When you don't play the same games they do, they notice that you are living by different rules. That's why they say such terrible things about you." (VOICE)

1 John 2:1-3 – "*You are* my little children, so I am writing these things to help you avoid sin. If, however, any believer does sin, we have a *high-powered* defense lawyer—Jesus the Anointed, the righteous—*arguing on our behalf* before the Father. It was through His sacrificial death that our sins were atoned. But He did not stop there—He died for the sins of the whole world. We know we have joined Him in an intimate relationship because we live out His commands." (VOICE)

THE ENCOUNTER THAT CHANGED ME FOREVER

There were so many situations I experienced during my 25-plus years in law enforcement. Many of these events were rewarding while others weren't. Of all those situations, my least favorite became the night when someone wanted to kill me simply because I wore a uniform and chose a profession that served and protected others. I never imagined I would have ever experienced that kind of encounter during my career. Unfortunately, I did, and it changed me forever.

It happened the night of Friday, August 22, 2008. I reported to work for my normal shift which began at 10 p.m. and ended at 6 a.m. the following morning. Around 10:15 p.m. we had just finished roll call, and I was putting myself into service.

The Greatest Gift Ever

About 10:20 p.m., two officers were dispatched to a residence for an unknown problem. Shortly after they arrived, they requested more units for what appeared to be a possible domestic instead.

Around 10:25 p.m., I arrived at their location and went to the rear of that residence. When I got to the back of the house, another officer was already in position. Soon more officers arrived on scene; some of them were detectives who were working a special detail nearby.

We were joined at the back of the residence by a detective. The three of us stayed there in case someone tried to run out the back door. While in the backyard, we noticed that a car was driving the wrong way down a one-way street. We shouted to the driver that they were going the wrong way, but they continued on. Officers out front finally made contact with the home's occupants, and after a brief encounter, all units were told to clear the call.

As we were departing, we were challenged by the driver of that car who drove the wrong way down that street. An enraged young man got out of the car yelling profanities at us. He then started walking to the rear of the residence we had just left.

The Encounter That Changed Me Forever

He continued cursing at us for being on his property as he walked away.

One of the other officers looked through the driver's side window into the car. Without warning, that same young man turned around and began walking back towards us. That officer yelled out that he saw a shotgun lying on the front seat inside the car.

I will never forget what happened next. It was like it happened yesterday. As he kept approaching us and without saying a word, that angry young man started to lift up his shirt with his left hand. I saw him reaching for a handgun he had hidden underneath his shirt in the front of his pants. I don't think I will ever forget the look in his eyes. It was a cold, dark, angry, blank, piercing stare. It was pure evil and pure hatred staring right at me. To this day, that look still haunts me sometimes.

Psalm 56:3-4 – "When struck by fear, I let go, depending *securely* upon You *alone*. In God—whose word I praise—in God I place my trust. I shall not let fear come in, for what can measly men do to me?" (VOICE)

I drew my weapon and started to fire it at him. Everything felt like it was all happening in slow motion. I don't remember hearing anything. Everything around me became blurry, and time seemed to just stand still. All I remember seeing was the front sight of my gun and a blurry image of the man, followed by a bright flash of light as I pulled the trigger, firing one round after another at him. Then everything became cloudy and foggy.

My sole goal right then and there was to make him stop what he was doing. I wanted to keep him from shooting one of us. I didn't want to die, and I didn't want any of my fellow officers to die, either. I just wanted him to go away and the whole nightmare to be over with. I wish it was all a bad dream, but it wasn't. I was in a fight for my life, and all because I wore a uniform and worked in a profession that had angered that young man to the point he wanted to kill me.

All my training kicked in during the incident. I don't remember firing my weapon until the magazine was empty, but I did. I don't remember firing while moving to cover, but somehow I did. I don't even remember reloading my weapon after I'd fired all of the bullets from my first magazine, but I did.

The Encounter That Changed Me Forever

The detective was to my left and a little behind me. The other officer was also to my left and further behind the detective. We were all positioned in a diagonal line. I was closest to that young man. He was about 20 feet in front when he reached for his gun and I began firing at him. He started to back up but was still facing us as he drew the gun with his right hand from his waistband.

As we exchanged gunfire, I saw the detective fall down face forward out of the corner of my left eye. I thought he'd been shot and screamed "officer down" over the radio, but to my shock and amazement, the detective got back up. He rose to his feet, and then I saw him falling down again, only this time backwards. Thinking he had been shot again, I yelled at him to stay down. I then proceeded to scream "officer down" over the radio again.

After the initial exchange of gunfire, the scene quickly became very chaotic. I didn't know if my two fellow officers were alive or dead. I didn't know the status of the suspect or where he was. I don't know how, but I found myself in a different position kneeling behind a nearby parked car when the gunfire stopped. Everything was so unclear, and the

The Greatest Gift Ever

radio was buzzing with all sorts of unrecognizable chatter. It was total chaos.

I started searching for the suspect in the immediate area when we quickly discovered that he was running away from the scene in the next street to our north. I started to run in that direction, and so many thoughts were running through my head. Every instinct I had inside of me was telling me to stop, but my duty to finish the job overrode those instincts and I kept running towards where the suspect was headed. When I arrived in the area, the suspect was nowhere to be found. As more and more units began arriving on the scene, we immediately started setting up a perimeter.

Not long after that, I was reunited with the two other officers. I was relieved and thankful, to say the least, that both of them were alive. Nobody had been shot. Once supervisors arrived on the scene, the three of us were pulled aside and directed to take them to the site where the initial exchange of gunfire occurred. Once the forensic unit arrived and began processing the shooting scene, the three of us were transported back to the police station one by one. This was all part of the standard protocol after an officer-involved shooting. The part I didn't like the

The Encounter That Changed Me Forever

most is when I had to surrender my weapon for processing. I don't know why it bothered me, but it just didn't sit too well with me, for whatever the reason.

Once I arrived back at the police station, I was isolated in a detective's office with the officer who transported me. Nobody said a word. There was just silence. Thus began one of the longest nights of my life. We were kept isolated until the county detectives arrived. They were now handling the shooting investigation.

As the night unfolded, I met with our Fraternal Order of Police union attorney and several other union representatives as well. During those meetings with the union personnel, I finally got the chance to call my family to let them know what happened and that I was okay. It was one of the hardest telephone calls I ever had to make. I didn't know what to say or how to say it. I doubt Lori even understood a word I said other than that I was okay.

As the initial shock of the whole thing began to slowly wear off, I remember becoming emotional as the reality of the whole situation became more and more apparent. I remember thinking to myself that I was grateful to be alive. I remember becoming angry that someone had tried to kill me. I remember the

The Greatest Gift Ever

horror when I thought that detective had been shot not only once but twice. There were so many things running through my mind that night. It was like wave after wave of up and down emotions.

While we were being processed at the police station, we learned that the suspect broke into a house near the scene after the shooting and was hiding in a second story bathroom. He called 911 because he had been shot several times and didn't want to bleed to death. He eventually surrendered to the county Crisis Response Team. While he was being treated at a nearby hospital, we were told that he'd been shot at least three times and had to undergo surgery for those wounds. Several hours later, we learned that he made it through the surgery and was recovering.

As the night progressed and the adrenaline began to wear off, I had a lot of pain and discomfort in my right shoulder. I could barely move it, and it seemed to become stiffer. I notified a supervisor of my possible injury. I was then transported to the hospital for treatment and released a few hours later. I was later told by the other officers that during the exchange of gunfire, I had fallen very hard on my right shoulder. From the pained look on my face, they thought I had also been shot but were relieved when they saw me get back up. Even though I didn't know it at the time, eventually I had to undergo surgery on that should for a partial rotator cuff tear and a few labrum tears.

My long night wrapped about 7 a.m. that Saturday morning. We were all scheduled to meet with the department's psychologist in just a few hours. In the meantime, we were told to go home and try to get some rest.

A few months after all the investigations into the shooting were completed, we were cleared by both our department and the District Attorney's Office as being justified in our decision to use deadly force during the incident. We learned that the suspect shot at us nine times without hitting one of us during the exchange of gunfire. We fired 22 times at him, hitting him three times in what turned out to be non-fatal wounds.

After the incident, I continued to struggle to comprehend the whole series of events. My emotions were out of control, and I know I wasn't dealing with things as well as I should have. I didn't understand God's role in all of it, and I questioned why God would even allow something like this to happen to one of His children. I know one of my issues with God stemmed from the fact that I'd not yet come full circle in my reconciliation with Him. I knew I'd begun that journey in New Jersey, but I was still a fragile work in progress.

During this time I continued to seek treatment from a psychologist who specialized in post-traumatic stress (PTSD) disorder. I discovered after our first meeting that not only was he a psychologist, but he was also a pastor. Jackpot! Throughout our following sessions, he walked me through my normal human responses to this traumatic event, but he also helped me to understand it all from a Christian perspective.

I had never before really believed in angels or fully understood to what lengths God would go to protect one of His children. We already know that I struggled in my past with having a solid belief in my salvation or that I was worthy of it to begin with. This psychologist not only helped me recover from my PTSD, but he also helped me recover spiritually from the whole incident.

The true miracle was that I came away from all of this with a new, stronger belief not only in my salvation but also in the fact that I was worthy of it all.

I finally started slowly laying down all my baggage and the belief that I had to earn my way into God's Kingdom. For the first time in my life, many of the pieces to the puzzle started to fit into place. I realized that I was a child of God, no matter what. In other words, no matter what I did after my salvation, I was and always would be a child of God. I had my reservation booked for eternal life with my God in heaven, no strings attached.

This was a huge step for me and helped me to positively move forward in my faith more than I ever had before. I finally had my burning bush and my miracle from God. I learned that on that particular night, I was confronted by something truly evil on a dark, lonely, desolate street. Something that wasn't of God; instead, it was something entirely from this world. Not only did angels protect me and my fellow officers, but God Himself also shielded us from any harm. I could hold my head up high. Humbly I could proclaim that, yes, I deserved God's protection because I belonged to God. I was His child. God was present that night, and He sent angels to help protect us. Even though I now realized I was forever a member of God's family, thankfully that night He wasn't calling me home just yet. Amen!

The Greatest Gift Ever

Psalm 140:1-2, 4-5 – "Save me, O Eternal One, from the evil men *who seek my life*. Shield me from *this band of* violent men. Their hearts devise evil! *They conspire against me;* they are constantly causing a storm of war. Keep me from the grip of these cruel *men,* O Eternal One. Shield me from *this band of* violent men whose *only* intention is to trip me up *and undermine all I do.* Those arrogant people are trying to catch me; they've laid their trap, hiding a net along my path; their traps are set, *and I am the prey.*" (VOICE)

This one traumatic event helped me to put both the incident and my whole life into perspective. This new perspective served me well during the subsequent trial after the shooting, when we learned why the young man wanted to kill us. Apparently he'd had an encounter earlier that night with the detectives on that special detail. Something happened during that encounter that made him very angry. He went home to his residence and had a fight with his girlfriend. He left there and got together with a few of his friends, and they conspired to kill a few cops — all because that young man was mad at the police.

The Encounter That Changed Me Forever

They called 911 knowing that the police would show up at his house. They were going to ambush the police after they arrived. Luckily, we got to his house before he did. One of his friends was supposed to take the shotgun from the car and lay in the bushes to shoot at the cops who went to the back of the house. Thankfully, that friend who chose to hide in the bushes intentionally left the shotgun in the car, instead.

We also learned during the trial that the young man, for some reason, had decided to commit "suicide by cop" that night. We almost became another statistic because he was mad at the police and wanted to kill some cops in retaliation. To make matters worse, initially he didn't plan to survive. He wanted us to end his life. I became the target of another man's anger because I had chosen to protect and serve.

A short time later during his sentencing hearing, we were given the opportunity to tell the judge how the whole incident had affected us. I never realized how much I was holding in until it was my turn to speak. I broke down when I began telling the judge what the incident had done to me. I tried to express how hurt I was that another human being wanted to kill me simply because of the uniform I wore. I could barely speak. I cried uncontrollably each time I attempted to utter a word. I couldn't stop crying, and I got extremely frustrated that I couldn't control my emotions. I even felt a little embarrassed. After all, cops aren't supposed to cry.

An Assistant District Attorney was present, and, to her credit, she helped me through the whole ordeal by consoling me as best she could. The man's family asked the court to be lenient based upon his unfortunate, terrible upbringing. He apparently suffered from a drug addiction and had some mental health issues as well.

My initial thoughts before the trial were that I wanted justice. I wanted him locked up forever for trying to kill me. I was angry, and I wanted to know that he would suffer for the rest of his life behind bars. That thought gave me great satisfaction.

Thankfully, God's plans and my subsequent transformation softened my heart before his sentencing. For the first time in my life, I looked at the whole incident through God's eyes instead of my own. The anger I once harbored inside instead transformed into love for another and genuine concern for that young man's well being. It took a lot, but I was able to forgive him, and I even told him I was glad he didn't die. That was truly a God thing and never something I imagined would have happened to me had God not been working behind the scenes.

I'll be the first one to tell you that in this line of work, you're a ticking time bomb if you don't know what the greatest gift ever is and you don't have your heart right. You'll lose it all, unless you're walking in harmony with God. Trust me, I know this first hand; been there, done that.

If the way I acted towards my family after my father's death wasn't enough to almost destroy everything, then my career in law enforcement almost certainly did. I, too, started going down that slippery slope that most cops go by shutting down both spiritually and emotionally while also trying in vain to keep all outsiders at arms length. Even though I was turning my life around in regards to my journey with my faith and my belief in God, I still hadn't completed that quest. To this day, I pray that God will always continue transforming me by helping me overcome all of my shortcomings.

If He can transform me, then I know that God will be faithful to transform you as well. All you have to do to start is always, unconditionally, give love to others, no matter what. This whole journey starts in your heart and moves outward from there in all that you say and do.

Matthew 5:44 – "But I say to you, Love your enemies and pray for those who persecute you," (NRSV)

Luke 6:27 – "But to you who are willing to listen, I say, love your enemies! Do good to those who hate you." (NLT)

Luke 6:35 – "Love your enemies! Do good to them. Lend to them without expecting to be repaid. Then your reward from heaven will be very great, and you will truly be acting as children of the Most High, for he is kind to those who are unthankful and wicked." (NLT)

WHY WE STRUGGLE

It might sound like a cliché, but it really couldn't be any easier to comprehend: the simple fact is that, in the end, we are human. We attach feelings and emotions to how we love. We see the world through our eyes instead of God's. Since we don't think like God, we don't consistently act Godly. We know right from wrong because we've been transformed, and the Holy Spirit resides in all of God's children who are born again; yet, we choose to do the very things we know we should not do. We want to change the circumstances behind every situation so the ultimate outcome is in our favor. We want to attach conditions and expiration dates to how long we'll continue doing something without seeing a return on our investment. We see the only way we'll ever be happy is to long for all those "things" we feel

God should have provided to us, instead of being satisfied with what we do have. We struggle with the fact that we are sinners. It's an endless, vicious circle, but one we can stop anytime we choose to do so.

We must transform our hearts and how we see if we're going to begin moving in the right direction. God loves those who are His children simply because His love for us is always unconditional with no strings attached. We don't have to try to continue to deserve His love. We don't have to constantly prove ourselves to Him to continue to receive His love. He doesn't stop loving us even though, in the end, we are all still sinners. God keeps on loving us unconditionally when we all know we don't deserve it. A simpler way of understanding this difference is this: ***<u>God always, unconditionally gives love to us, no matter what, without expecting anything in return</u>***. No "ifs," "ands," or "buts" attached. How many of us can truly say we are consistently doing the same right now?

The key to understanding what is truly God's love requires us to no longer "see" love through human eyes but, instead, to transform spiritually to see love through God's eyes. Until we make this new way of seeing an essential part of our spiritual journey, we'll continually fail to fully comprehend what Godly love is. Seeing through God's eyes will also begin to change our journey with God. Just as with changing our hearts, to walk in harmony with God means we must also begin to see love through God's eyes instead of our own.

*Always, unconditionally giving love to others by **seeing** through God's eyes, no matter what, becomes a crucial element in completing your transformation.*

Until we learn this, we'll continue to struggle to overcome all of our other issues that are holding us back. I believe you can't overcome the issue of surrendering all to God until you learn to always, unconditionally give love to others. I believe we cannot overcome the issue of sin or forgiveness until we learn to always, unconditionally give love to others. I also believe you'll never overcome letting go of your past until you finally learn to always, unconditionally give love to others, no matter what.

We could continue to add any number of other issues that we might be suffering from to the list.

The Greatest Gift Ever

These could include envy, lust, hate, anger, depression, loss, frustration, bitterness, guilt, etc. Once you begin to always, unconditionally give love not only to God but also to God's people and God's world, then the true miracle of maturing in your walk through your Christian faith will begin your ultimate transformation into being more like Christ.

I'm not saying that this is a one size fits all remedy. It's a step by step process. Each person's situation is unique. Only you know where you are spiritually, both presently or in your past. However, if you allow God, Christ, and the Holy Spirit to begin this amazing transformation, starting with your heart, then you, too, will begin to see through God's eyes the miracle of what always, unconditionally giving love to others, no matter what, looks like. You'll finally comprehend why God's love is the greatest gift ever. That knowledge will set you free to soar towards your ultimate goal of becoming more like Christ.

Remember: God already always, unconditionally loves you, no matter what you've done or continue to do. The greatest gift ever has and always will be yours. You can't exchange it, and you can't give it back. It belongs to you no matter who you were or who you choose to become. (In other words, you can't lose your salvation.)

Isaiah 55:6-7 – "Look for the Lord while He may be found. Call upon Him while He is near. Let the sinful turn from his way, and the one who does not know God turn from his thoughts. Let him turn to the Lord, and He will have loving-pity on him. Let him turn to our God, for He will for sure forgive all his sins." (NLV)

2 Corinthians 5:17 – "Therefore, if anyone *is* in Christ, *he is* a new creation; old things have passed away; behold, all things have become new." (NKJV)

NO MORE EXCUSES

I know there are other Christians who will disagree with me on the salvation issue, and that's okay. We can't all agree on everything. In fact I remember vividly during one Bible study on Anderson's book when half the class was split down the middle on the issue of whether or not you can lose your salvation once you have it. Half the group felt that you could lose your salvation and that you had to constantly live your life earning it. The other half of the class believed the same as I do: once saved, always saved. Here's something to keep in mind: in addition to always, unconditionally giving love to you, no matter what, God already knows and sees what lies in your heart. You'll continue to struggle to understand your salvation if you keep trying to view it from your eyes instead of God's. Likewise, until you stop attaching your feelings and emotions to it all, you will continue to struggle to fully comprehend why God always, unconditionally gives love to you, no matter what.

The simple truth in all of this is that Satan will always try to obtain a foothold in you. He will use any foothold he can to keep you separated from God. Your struggle to fully comprehend God's love for you and your salvation is the very reason Satan desires to keep his foothold in you. Satan wants you to keep viewing love through your human eyes instead of seeing the truth through God's eyes. His goal is to keep us from growing closer to God. Without any foothold, Satan has no power over you.

John 8:44 – "For you are the children of your father the devil, and you love to do the evil things he does. He was a murderer from the beginning. He has always hated the truth, because there is no truth in him. When he lies, it is consistent with his character; for he is a liar and the father of lies." (NLT)

Romans 16:20 – "The God of peace will soon crush Satan under your feet. The grace of our Lord Jesus be with you." (NIV)

James 4:7 – "Submit yourselves, then, to God. Resist the devil, and he will flee from you." (NIV)

Never forget that Satan exists and that he'll do whatever he can to separate you from God. He wants nothing more than to keep your mind fixed on seeing things with earthly eyes instead of with Godly eyes. Satan will constantly try to deceive you; he's relentless, and you'll always be under attack. His only mission is to separate you from God. But with the Godly tools we receive with our salvation, each of us has the ability to choose not to fall for Satan's deceit any longer.

One of Satan's greatest tools is deceiving us into believing God's love and our salvation came with strings attached. Satan wants you to continue in your "stinkin' thinkin'." He'll use every trick and lie at his disposal. He'll never stop and will constantly attack us, especially when we're weakest. In the end we're our own worst enemy, responsible for our own lack of growth. Start loving as God loves. Start seeing yourself as God already sees you. Stand fast in the belief that God always, unconditionally gives love to you, no matter what, and then you'll be free from any foothold Satan is trying to gain inside you.

Colossians 1:13 – "For he has rescued us from the dominion of darkness and brought us into the kingdom of the Son he loves, ..." (NIV)

1 John 5:18 – "We know that anyone born of God does not continue to sin; the One who was born of God keeps them safe, and the evil one cannot harm them." (NIV)

Another sad truth, especially in present times, is that our world is constantly trying to convince us into believing that we can live apart from God. Being a Christian comes with the understanding that there are absolute truths. Clearly, that understanding is crucial in our goal of adopting a wholly Biblical view of our world today.

Christian pollster George Barna conducted an extensive poll in the U.S. on the prevalence of what he referred to as a Biblical worldview. He defined someone as having a Biblical worldview when they believed that the Bible is totally accurate in all of the principles it teaches; that Satan is considered to be a real being or force, not merely symbolic; that a person cannot earn their way into Heaven by trying to be good or do good works; that Jesus Christ lived a sinless life on earth; and that God is the all-knowing, all-powerful creator of the world Who still rules the universe today.

The results of his study were shocking, to say the least. Only 9% of American adults polled possessed a Biblical worldview. Even more disturbing was that only 19% of those who claimed to be born again possessed a Biblical worldview. That is very troublesome. Those statistics, especially for people claiming to be born again, emphasize a need for immediate change.

Another area that reflects our society's growing belief in living independently from God can be found in the recent Supreme Court ruling that changed forever the definition of marriage in this country. To avoid a huge debate with my readers, and I'm not trying to offend others, suffice it to say I believe in God's foundation for traditional marriage.

Marriage was given to us by God. No human court of law has the right to define what marriage is. I believe that traditional marriage has always involved the union between God, one man, and one woman. I also believe that marriage involves fulfilling that covenant from that day forward, no matter what.

The disturbing results regarding some of the recent marriage statistics in our society concern me greatly. In October 2012 the McKinley Irvin Family Law organization posted the following divorce statistics, according to the U.S. Census Bureau. The divorce rate for 1st marriages was 41%; for 2nd marriages the rate increased to 60%; and for 3rd marriages, the rate was a jaw-dropping 73%. Even more disturbing was that a divorce occurs approximately every 36 seconds in our country. That equates to nearly 2,400 divorces per day, 16,800 divorces per week, and nearly 876,000 divorces annually in the U.S. The average age of a person going through their 1st divorce was 30, and the average length of a marriage ending in divorce was eight years.

I find it interesting that you can receive a diploma after graduating from an educational institute you attended, which included writing papers and passing several tests over an extended period of time. To receive a driver's license for the first time, you have to study a book and then pass both a written and a driving road test. We have certifications you must obtain before you can work in many professions, such as plumber, electrician, or even police officer. You must first pass a background check to

The Greatest Gift Ever

legally own a gun in our country before completing the purchase. Heck, even lawyers have to graduate from law school and then pass the bar before being allowed to practice. Yet, we aren't required to attend any classes, write any papers, practice, study, pass a test, or even pass a background check to receive a marriage license in this great country.

If all that wasn't enough to concern me about our society's attempt to convince us to live apart from God, what about the fact that our country was founded based upon a belief in God and religion? Our very constitution and the constitutions of all 50 states refer to God and religion, which is how America became so great. The very fabric of our nation was sewn with principles derived from the Bible. America has attracted people from all over the world from generation to generation because of those principles that have made us who we are. People have flocked from the ends of the earth to become citizens of a country that promotes equality and freedom for all.

Did you know that on January 25, 1988, Congress mandated that the first Thursday of every May would be known as a National Day of Prayer? That wasn't even 20 years ago, yet today there seems to be an ever-growing sentiment among Americans towards living apart from God. It seems that our countrymen desire to live life their way, instead of holding onto those same religious beliefs that founded this great country of ours.

How, then, could we ever be fooled into believing that we could ever possibly live without God? Whether it's having faith, possessing a Biblical worldview, traditional marriage, or remembering the Godly principles that laid the foundation for our great nation, believing that you can live apart from God is no way to live at all. Trust me: been there, done that and failed miserably. If you're a member of God's family, then you especially can't live without Him. He is always inside of you, and that won't ever change. You can try, but sooner or later God will get your attention. He always wins in the end. Wouldn't it be easier for you in the long run to do your best to follow God's plan for your life, instead of trying to fool yourself that you don't have to?

Psalm 19:8 – "The Laws of the Lord are right, giving joy to the heart. The Word of the Lord is pure, giving light to the eyes." (NLV)

The Greatest Gift Ever

Psalm 23:1-3 – "The Lord *is* my shepherd; I shall not want. He makes me to lie down in green pastures; He leads me beside the still waters. He restores my soul; He leads me in the paths of righteousness For His name's sake." (NKJV)

A few years ago, Lori gave me a religious daily devotional desk calendar that sits proudly on top of my dresser in our bedroom. A devotion is written for every day throughout the year. One of the more recent ones to grab my attention lately was from an unknown author who recited these amazing words:

"To know the will of God is the greatest knowledge, to find the will of God is the greatest discovery, to do the will of God is the greatest achievement."

Does that at all describe where you find yourself today in your own Christian walk? Don't be too hard on yourself if that statement doesn't reflect where you are in your journey just yet. I believe that if you have already chosen to always give love to others, no matter what, that will pave the way for you accomplish so many wonderful things in your life. Take solace in the fact that finding, knowing, and doing the will of God will result in you achieving the greatest discovery, knowledge, and achievement you could ever possibly obtain for yourself.

Psalm 34:15,17 – "The eyes of the Lord are on those who do what is right and good. His ears are open to their cry. Those who are right with the Lord cry, and He hears them. And He takes them from all their troubles." (NLV)

Proverbs 15:3 – "The eyes of the Lord are in every place, keeping watch on the evil and the good." (NRSV)

SEEING THROUGH GOD'S EYES

―⦻⦻⦻―

For myself, I guess it boiled down to the simple fact that because I'm not God, how could I ever hope to learn to see things through His eyes? I'm only human, after all, and it was always hard for me to freely give love to someone who, according to my own feelings and emotions, had done nothing to deserve it. Isn't that the very core of our human understanding of love? Isn't our love for others based upon both parties giving and receiving? I mean, we don't just don't unconditionally give love to someone; they have to earn it first, right? Not to mention the fact that if they don't "give love to" me in return, then it's only fair that I withhold my love for them until I get something back. Makes sense, right? Not really.

It was very hard for me not to think and feel that way, especially during the crucial early years of my marriage. Having a faulty notion of what love truly was repeatedly became a huge stumbling block for me throughout my life. I clung to that worldly notion that love centered on both giving **and receiving**. Kind of like believing that I do because they did, or even along the lines of tit for tat. As you can imagine, that sort of stinkin' thinkin' didn't always work out the best for me in the end. It caused way too many arguments between Lori and me, way more than it should have.

Don't worry, you aren't a failure, and you certainly aren't alone if you felt that way. It's okay. Here's the kicker. At this very moment, it's time to change your view on this whole love concept. We all know now that the greatest gift ever is God's love for those who are His children. It also goes much deeper than that. Not only must you believe that God already unconditionally loves you, but you're then also required to unconditionally give love to others.

I believe that the only way we can accomplish that feat is by learning to see things as our God sees them. We have to learn to act from our Christian hearts, allowing God to guide us instead of relying on our worldly views of things. We who call ourselves children of God have been given all the tools we need to transform ourselves into what God wants us to be. We have numerous examples to follow from the Bible about how we need to learn to freely and unconditionally give love not only to our God but also to others. There are also numerous examples of the consequences of **not** learning to love as God loves. After Jesus' crucifixion and eventual ascension into heaven, we received the Holy Spirit, another amazing free gift. The Holy Spirit will guide you to help you follow God's plan for your life. Think of it as having a moral compass; when you come to a crossroads, you'll know which path to take if you're letting the Holy Spirit lead you and light the path beneath your feet.

I truly believe that if you learn to utilize all the tools in your Christian tool belt that God has supplied, then your subsequent transformation into learning how to love as God already loves you and seeing things as God sees them will finally begin. I'm not saying that this transformation and your journey that follows after you begin always, unconditionally giving love to others will ever be an easy one. Make no mistake, there will be constant obstacles, distractions, difficulties, and a lot of pain you'll have to inevitably endure. I don't doubt that the rewards you'll begin to experience along the path of your journey through life will make all the obstacles you may encounter much easier to cope with. Conversely, you'll also undoubtedly also experience many highs along your journey and, hopefully, experience your own series of "from God ah ha" moments along your way.

I know you'll find all of your highs and lows to be worth it in the end. I can't think of a better place to be than living in harmony with God, as opposed to choosing to just get by and hang on through all of those bumps in the road. God desires to live in harmony with every one of His children. All you must do to also have a close harmonious relationship with God and ensure your place in Heaven is to choose to spend time with Him daily. Force yourself to put down your smartphone, turn off the television, and tune out all the other distractions. Sit in silence, dust off your Bible, and spend some time reading God's word. Meditate on all the new concepts God reveals to you. Start to frequently pray to Him. Make it a habit. Pray to God for the strength you need to transform. Seek wisdom, fruit of the Spirit, and all the Godly virtues as expressed in 1 Corinthians 13.

The Greatest Gift Ever

Strive to find, know, and do God's will in your daily life, and you'll soon reap many great rewards.

There are several resources available that will assist you with your desire to spend more quality time with God. One of the most rewarding ways I found that helped me to become closer to God was by reading daily devotional books. Most are filled with stories from people who are sharing their experiences similar to your own regarding the highs and lows they encountered during their Christian journey. No matter what resource you choose to use, keep focused on your desire to grow closer to God. Don't forget to take time to listen during those moments when you're in the midst of being still and quiet. Soon you, too, will begin to hear God's gentle voice calling out to you. From there you'll begin to understand the perfect plan He has in store for you.

Proverbs 3:6 – "In all your ways acknowledge Him, And He will make your paths straight." (NASB)

Isaiah 50:10 – "*So,* you who are listening, do you acknowledge the Eternal One *as God*? And do you take seriously what the servant of God has to say? If you are enveloped in darkness, with no light *to see*, take confidence in the name of the Eternal One; rely on your God." (VOICE)

Jeremiah 17:5, 7 – "This is what the LORD says: 'Cursed is the one who trusts in man, who draws strength from mere flesh and whose heart turns away from the LORD. But blessed is the one who trusts in the LORD, whose confidence is in him.' " (NIV)

BEGIN THE TRANSFORMATION

There is no magic formula, pill, or quick remedy that will cause you to change. You'll change because you decide to do so. If you're a child of God, then you must begin to change, and the sooner the better. Don't wait until tomorrow. Make the decision to change. Right here, right now. No more excuses, no more conditions, no more date stamps, and definitely no more "ifs, ands, or buts."

Besides, now that you're armed with a new understanding of Godly love, won't choosing to change prove to be a much better choice in the long run than continuing to go through life as you are now? If you take any hope away from the many "from God ah ha" moments I've experienced, I'm sure as time goes on you'll encounter your own "from God ah ha" moments, too. My only words of advice for those moments are to be careful what you wish for.

Galatians 2:20 – "I have been crucified with Christ and I no longer live, but Christ lives in me. The life I now live in the body, I live by faith in the Son of God, who loved me and gave himself for me." (NIV)

Don't become discouraged, and never give up. This will be a long process and most certainly will be highlighted by many victories and defeats. Thankfully, because of the growth in my relationship with God, He began this inspiration in which I finally understood what this greatest gift ever was all about. Don't fool yourself by thinking for an instant that your journey forward won't be challenging. It will. It always will.

John 16:27 – "… for the Father Himself loves you, because you have loved Me, and have believed that I came forth from God." (NKJV)

That might be a little discouraging to some. Yet for others, like me, I hope that, as I learn to always, unconditionally give love to others, as my God already does, then, with His help, coupled with my faith and the gift of the Holy Spirit, I, too, will begin to transform. I will slowly begin to grow closer to my God by learning to always, unconditionally give my love to others.

1 John 4:13-15 – "By this we know that we abide in Him and He in us, because He has given us of His Spirit. We have seen and testify that the Father has sent the Son *to be* the Savior of the world. Whoever confesses that Jesus is the Son of God, God abides in him, and he in God." (NASB)

1 John 5:1 – "The person who believes that Jesus is the Christ is a child of God. The person who loves the Father loves His children also." (NLV)

1 John 5:3 – "Loving God means to obey His Word, and His Word is not hard to obey." (NLV)

In this next section, I'll give you four steps that will help you become the person God created you to be, based on my life experiences and what's worked for me.

Step One – *loving God*

So why is it so important for us to understand this concept about what it truly means to unconditionally give love to others? I believe that ***comprehending this concept is the first step to our continued growth in our faith and, ultimately, to our beginning to live in harmony with God***. Without comprehending the true meaning of what love is and understanding what love isn't, we'll continue to struggle and fail to fully complete our transformation. You won't successfully achieve the goal of learning to live as we were meant to by striving to become more Christ-like every day. I can't stress this point enough. Think about it. How could we ever hope that others would ever truly see God in us if we're not first, unconditionally giving love to others? After all, God is love, and we can't say we know God without first unconditionally giving love to Him. As we've discussed previously, not only is Godly love the greatest gift ever, but it is also the greatest commandment, according to Jesus.

Matthew 22:37-38 – "He said to him, 'You shall love the Lord your God with all your heart, and with all

The Greatest Gift Ever

---

your soul, and with all your mind.' This is the greatest and first commandment." (NRSV)

There you have it. Straight from Jesus' lips, our greatest and most important commandment is to "love our God" with "all" that we have in our hearts, souls, and minds. You're commanded to always, unconditionally give love to God with everything you have, no matter what.

Deuteronomy 6:5-7 – "You shall love the Lord your God with all your heart and with all your soul and with all your might. These words, which I am commanding you today, shall be on your heart. You shall teach them diligently to your sons and shall talk of them when you sit in your house and when you walk by the way and when you lie down and when you rise up." (NASB)

Mark 12:30 – "You must love the Lord your God with all your heart and with all your soul and with all your mind and with all your strength. This is the first Law." (NLV)

This all might seem like an impossible task to achieve. At times during your Christian journey, you're right, it will, but remember that God has given you all the tools necessary for you to begin your transformation once you were born again. You have your faith and the Holy Spirit to guide you, as well as the knowledge that you're capable of giving to others the Godly love that now resides inside of you. You have all you need to embark on this incredible journey of fulfilling your greatest and most important commandment.

If you have never made the decision to join God's family, make that decision, right here, right now, by reciting the following conversion prayer out loud: Heavenly Father, I know I am a sinner and I ask for Your forgiveness. I believe, Jesus Christ is the Son of the living God, that He died for my sins, and that God raised Christ from the dead. I ask you into my heart, to become my Lord, and Savior. I ask these things in Christ's name, Amen.

Romans 10:9-10 – "If you declare with your mouth, 'Jesus is Lord,' and believe in your heart that God raised him from the dead, you will be saved. For it is with your heart that you believe and are justified, and it is with your mouth that you profess your faith and are saved." (NIV)

Congratulations! You have just made the most important decision in your life to follow Jesus. I encourage you to consult with a pastor as soon as possible before continuing on with this book.

Galatians 5:16-17 – "So I say, let the Holy Spirit guide your lives. Then you won't be doing what your sinful nature craves. The sinful nature wants to do evil, which is just the opposite of what the Spirit wants. And the Spirit gives us desires that are the opposite of what the sinful nature desires. These two forces are constantly fighting each other, so you are not free to carry out your good intentions." (NLT)

Jude 1:19-21 – "These are the people who divide you, who follow mere natural instincts and do not have the Spirit. But you, dear friends, by building yourselves up in your most holy faith and praying in the Holy Spirit, keep yourselves in God's love as you wait for the mercy of our Lord Jesus Christ to bring you to eternal life." (NIV)

Step Two – *loving others*

Where do we go from here? What then becomes our next step to change? Look no further than what Jesus gave us as ***our second greatest commandment***.

Matthew 22:39-40 – "The second is like it, 'You must love your neighbor as you love yourself.' All the Laws and the writings of the early preachers depend on these two most important Laws." (NLV)

Again, it doesn't get any clearer than that. According to Jesus, after you love God with all your heart, mind, and soul, you're then called upon to also always, unconditionally give love to others, in this case your neighbor, no matter what. Wow, what a simple, yet complex, commandment.

Why does this commandment seem to be another insurmountable hurdle impeding our progress towards our ultimate transformation to become more Christ-like? I wish there were a simple answer, but I'm sure we could find as many answers as we could also find excuses. For me, it probably boiled down to the fact that this commandment goes against our very nature as humans. It goes back to the point of why should we ever give something to someone else without getting something in return. The good old notion of "tit for tat," or I did, so they must also do.

Romans 13:10 – "Love does no wrong to others, so love fulfills the requirements of God's law." (NLT)

I don't know about you, but that last Bible verse is interesting, only because, before I began working on Step One – which was followed by the even more challenging Step Two – I was unable to fully comprehend its true meaning. After all, I'm human, and there was no way I would just always, unconditionally give my love to others without getting something in return.

I've shared the many examples in my life where I struggled to understand what Godly love really was, as opposed to what I thought it meant. The simple, hard truth is that, without beginning to transform yourself by first tackling loving God first and then loving others second, you'll be unable to complete your transformation. Just as with each of the basic elements contained within God's whole love blueprint, these steps also build upon each other and are dependent on each other in order for you to successfully transform. You will continually be stuck in a never-ending cycle of conflict between doing what you're called to do because you're a child of God and what you "feel" like doing. That, my friend, again boils down to more "stinkin' thinkin'." You'll continue to set yourself up for failure by not completing your transformation. Once you begin, don't ever quit, and don't ever give up. It won't be easy and will always be a challenge, but it's all worth it in the end. Keep your eyes on the prize.

Ephesians 4:1-3 – "Therefore I, the prisoner of the Lord, implore you to walk in a manner worthy of the calling with which you have been called, with all humility and gentleness, with patience, showing tolerance for one another in love, being diligent to preserve the unity of the Spirit in the bond of peace." (NASB)

Step Three – *surrendering all of you to God*

This leads us to our next crucial step along our journey to transformation. Bear with me for just a

The Greatest Gift Ever

moment as I again share with you a glimpse of my past to help better illustrate my point.

Lori would be the first to tell you that previously I was a proud, confident, and even often at times, a very arrogant person. That's kind of harsh coming from your wife, but she's totally correct. Then again, that's who I learned to be growing up. Many times before and, unfortunately, even after I became a child of God, my pride, arrogance, and confidence in my own abilities resulted in a lot of unnecessary turmoil in my life. I know you're all saying it can't be so, but it's true. I'm sure many of you have heard the term "Type A" personality … that would exactly describe my personality to a tee.

That personality served its purpose at various times during my life. It was something that helped first attract Lori to me. It enabled me to meet new people and make friends easily. It made me a "go getter" and "hard charger" while I served in the military. My personality helped me to effortlessly display the many natural leadership qualities and instincts I possessed, which subsequently allowed me to serve in several very high profile positions that resulted in my quick rise up through the ranks. I know that my personality served me well and made me a very effective criminal investigator and police officer. Even though my personality served me well early in life, it was probably the single, biggest obstacle I faced in truly transforming into the Christian, husband, and man God called me to be. Why? I'm so glad you asked.

If I had to sum it up in one word, "surrender" definitely comes to mind. In the beginning, my inability to willingly surrender "all of me" to God and allow Him to help me transform into what He called me to be was huge. I never realized it at the time, but my inability to surrender was probably the single, biggest obstacle in front of me that was responsible for many of the highs and lows I experienced during my Christian journey. It wasn't something I was doing intentionally, and for the most part, I was unaware that I hadn't already surrendered it all to my God.

No, that truth came to light many years after I was saved. The frustrating part for me was that when God made me aware that I hadn't fully surrendered it all to Him, for some reason I still chose to disobedient. I don't know why I was so reluctant. Probably some doubt was to blame, but I think it was more than just that. I believe that because of my personality, deep down inside I felt that somehow giving it all to Him would turn me into something else; that, somehow, I might become a weaker man, or someone I didn't know, or maybe even into becoming something I couldn't ever possibly be.

Part of my hesitancy came from my lack of understanding who I was in Christ. Not only didn't I know what my role was after I became saved, but I also never truly understood who my God was. That so-called Christian identity crisis was something I would struggle with for many years. Today, I have no doubt that I would have handled many situations differently, especially my marriage and my father's death, had I better understood those concepts sooner.

Thankfully, there is a resource available that will help guide you through this process if you, too, struggle as I did with those very same concepts. I previously referred to it as Christianity 101 or even "Christianity for Dummies." Whatever it means to you, I can't stress to you enough the importance of you also reading Anderson's *Victory Over the Darkness: Realize the Power of Your Identity in Christ*. In addition to learning how to spend daily time with my God, this study helped me start my long-overdue transformation. My hope and prayer for all of you who read this book is that it, too, will provide you with the necessary instructions you need to help get you where you need to be. You won't be sorry, and I challenge all of you to discover that for yourselves.

Okay, so back to my surrender issue. I'm not sure how, where, or when I did fully surrender "all of me" to God. I believe I took several baby steps before that moment when God knocked me down to my hands and knees that I previously shared several chapters ago. I can look back at my life now and realize that there were many experiences and situations where my lack of total surrender should have been a lot more evident to me.

All of those events should have been an eye opener for me. If that wasn't frustrating enough, there were also several, what I like to refer to now as "the gentle knock on my door from God" moments that should have gotten my attention.

What do I mean by God's gentle knock? Simply this: I believe that God gives us the freedom to choose our paths at various times during our Christian journey. I liken it to when you come to a crossroads. You can no longer just go straight. You're sitting there pondering whether to turn left or turn right. Which way to choose? You feel "led"

The Greatest Gift Ever

---

that God wants you to turn right, but instead, for whatever reason, you ultimately turn left. It may take some time or maybe you're lucky enough that you realize instantly that you've made the wrong choice. Either way, God wanted you to go the one way, but you chose instead to go the other way for whatever reason.

No worries. God in His infinite wisdom will bring you back to that very same crossroads. But again, you struggle with which way to turn. You know which way you went last time and how it all worked out for you yet you still struggle to take God's path instead of your own.

I have come to believe that unless you're living in harmony with God, unfortunately you'll always choose to take the wrong path when you come to these crossroads in your life. The reasoning behind your decision and the many excuses you can make for your decision won't ever truly justify your choice. Maybe you also struggle with many of the same issues I experienced during my own journey, or maybe you're facing some very different issues altogether. Maybe you're struggling by choosing not to always, unconditionally give love to others, by failing to surrender to God, or by suffering from constant sin, a lack of forgiveness, pride, arrogance, or even anger. Your list could be endless, but that isn't the point. Whether or not your crossroads is new or one that you've previously visited, more likely than not you'll choose the wrong path unless you're living in harmony with God. You'll never have that peace until you first learn to always, unconditionally give love to God, then give that same Godly love back to others, and then surrendering all of you to God.

I'm not making light of those times when we each have chosen to follow the wrong path. But it's completely frustrating to me when I look back at all those times when I repeatedly chose the wrong path. Even though I'd been to that crossroads before and knew exactly what perils lay ahead, over and over again I still chose to go the wrong way. Talk about continuing to bang your head against the wall! You'd think that at some point I'd have just said, "Ouch! that hurts," and finally listened to God's voice by taking His path instead of my own.

I have shared with you the many hurdles and obstacles I have faced during my own journey and walk with God. Each time I rose to the challenge and felt I had finally moved in the direction God wanted me to, I soon realized that there was always more to do. There were times I chose to move in the right direction, and there were many times God forced me into that direction because I wasn't following His plan. Either way, whenever I finally figured out I was no longer on a level playing field with God, circumstances arose that made me take on that next challenge and continue with my transformation.

It should be the same for you. Don't ever settle for staying stationary. There is always more to learn. You have an unlimited ability to learn more than you could have possibly ever realized. Keep growing in your Godly love and faith. Just getting by shouldn't be good enough anymore. Trust me. Been there done that. Don't put a ceiling on top of your relationship with God. Your journey with God should always be limitless as the sky is above your head.

Psalm 31:3 – "Since you are my rock and my fortress, for the sake of your name lead and guide me." (NIV)

Psalm 145:13 – "Thy kingdom is an everlasting kingdom, And thy dominion *endureth* throughout all generations." (ASV)

Romans 5:1 – "Now that we have been made right with God by putting our trust in Him, we have peace with Him. It is because of what our Lord Jesus Christ did for us." (NLV)

Step Four – *leave your past behind*

Now we've come to an area of our lives where we'll all struggle from time to time, some more than others, and yet, some of us are still unable to move past this step. What am I talking about? Josh Wilson's song "That Was Then, This Is Now" sums it up best for me. We need to "go ahead, put the past in the past, box it up like an old photograph." Easier said than done, right? Of course it is.

Why will we all find this step to be such a challenge? Again our reasons and excuses are numerous, but I believe it all comes back again to our being human. We will constantly struggle to let our past go, especially those experiences that are very painful and hurt us the most. I know when I've been hurt or perceived I'd been wronged by someone, I wanted that instant satisfaction of watching that person also suffer "something" in return. Not tomorrow, next week, next month, or next year. What I believed that would also make me feel even better was being lucky enough to witness their suffering first hand. Thankfully, God doesn't allow us to have our cake and eat it too.

2 Corinthians 2:11 – "We forgive so that Satan will not win. We know how he works!" (NLV)

Colossians 3:13 – "Make allowance for each other's faults, and forgive anyone who offends you. Remember, the Lord forgave you, so you must forgive others." (NLT)

Your transformation progress will be affected if you don't let go of the past and leave it in the past. The catch, along with burying your shortcomings, failures, hurts, pains, and disappointments, is that you must also forgive those who were responsible for it. No, it isn't easy. None of these steps is easy. If this were easy, would it be worth doing? Now, I'm not saying that we should never remember our past. Your past experiences made you into who you are today.

By now you'll see a pattern developing here. Each step is unique and serves its own purpose to help you to begin to change. Independent from each other, they won't motivate you to change. But together they allow you build upon your more solid Godly love foundation and pave the way for you to begin living in harmony with God. Unfortunately, failing to complete any part of the process will not allow you to truly become the Christian who God has called you to be.

Matthew 7:24-27 – "Therefore everyone who hears these words of mine and puts them into practice is like a wise man who built his house on the rock. The rain came down, the streams rose, and the winds blew and beat against the house; yet it did not fall, because it had its foundation on the rock. But everyone who hears these words of mine and does not put them into practice is like a foolish man who built his house on sand. The rain came down, the streams rose, and the winds blew and beat against that house, and it fell with a great crash." (NIV)

NEW BEGINNINGS

Now that you know God's love is the greatest gift ever and how you're called upon to always, unconditionally give love to others, no matter what, what will each new day be like for you? Choosing to transform into living more like Christ will never be easy, and it will probably take you the rest of your life to perfect, but that shouldn't stop you from trying.

Imagine your world and how it could change if, starting within your own heart, you allowed Godly love to transform you. What would your world look like through your new sense of seeing by choosing to always, unconditionally giving love to others, no matter what? Would others also be able to see God in you? Can you see God in them? Take a few minutes now to write down your answers to those questions. What do your answers to those questions reveal to you?

Think about it. Wouldn't you then live in a truly perfect world when you finally see everything through God's eyes and not your own? What would that world now look like? What would that world finally feel like to live in? What if you chose to simplify everything and, instead, viewed your world differently for just one day? Can you imagine the changes that would occur all around you if you started with just one day at a time, and then let God take it from there?

1 Corinthians 15:51-54 – "For sure, I am telling you a secret. We will not all die, but we will all be changed. In a very short time, no longer than it takes for the eye to close and open, the Christians who have died will be raised. It will happen when the last horn sounds. The dead will be raised never to die again. Then the rest of us who are alive will be changed. Our human bodies made from dust must be changed into a body that cannot be destroyed. Our human bodies that can die must be changed into bodies that will never die. When this that can be destroyed has been changed into that which cannot be destroyed, and when this that does die has been changed into that which cannot die, then it will happen as the Holy Writings said it would happen. They said, 'Death has no more power over life.' " (NLV)

1 Corinthians 15:57 – "But God is the One Who gives us power over sin through Jesus Christ our Lord. We give thanks to Him for this." (NLV)

2 Corinthians 2:14 – "But thanks be to God, who always leads us in triumph in Christ, and manifests through us the sweet aroma of the knowledge of Him in every place." (NASB)

2 Corinthians 3:18 – "So all of us who have had that veil removed can see and reflect the glory of the Lord. And the Lord—who is the Spirit—makes us more and more like him as we are changed into his glorious image." (NLT)

The Perfect Day

If you're like most of us in today's world, you feel as though you're running a never-ending race to have enough hours in your day to get everything done you feel needs to be done. Exhausting, isn't it? Ever win that race, even if it was just one day? If you answered that question truthfully, it was most likely a resounding "No!".

Ever experience one of those days when you wake up with every intention of making the day different from the one before? You know the day I'm talking about, that so-called perfect day we all hope for, like the one when, instead of sleeping in, you get up and exercise like an Olympic athlete. Or maybe you wake up early and make your family a gourmet breakfast fit for a king. Maybe your perfect day starts with finally leaving the house early for work so you aren't driving like the Roadrunner to make it there on time. Like most of us, we've all experienced a day that didn't turn out the way we'd hoped.

What about that amazing day when you leave all the baggage behind that you've been carrying around all your life? The baggage will be different for each of us. For some, it's not forgiving someone who wronged us. For many, it may be depression. Could it be regret? What about the many disappointments we've experienced over the years? Maybe it's anger. For others, it could be the loss of a loved one.

The Greatest Gift Ever

The list could be endless. The bottom line is, what would a day without any of those issues feel like?

Maybe you strive for that perfect day with God. You spend time reading His word in the Bible instead of flipping through your smartphone. Instead of channel surfing with your television remote control, you spend time praying to God. For others, it may consist of spending time in meditation with God instead of wasting time on the Internet. Maybe your perfect day is one when you start and finish the day with God as your focal point. For most of us that perfect day might be the one when we simply choose not to sin.

Now think about the many different relationships we all have experienced. What if our perfect day merely consisted of doing our part regarding those relationships? Maybe it's spending time with your children, or maybe you choose to do something special for your spouse, not because you have to but because you want to. It could be as simple as treating everyone you encounter that day the way you're supposed to.

Taking things a step further, imagine a day when you decide to do all the right things "just because." Like driving to work and allowing the car next to you room to merge, instead of speeding up and cutting them off. Don't laugh. I know you know you've done it, and probably even on more than once. Or not tailgating the car in front of you? Did you hold that door open for someone coming into the building behind you, even if they were a few seconds away?

John 17:23 – "I in them, and You in Me; that they may be made perfect in one, and that the world may know that You have sent Me, and have loved them as You have loved Me." (NKJV)

1 John 4:17 – "By this, love is perfected with us, so that we may have confidence in the day of judgment; because as He is, so also are we in this world." (NASB)

A Perfect World

To truly see another human being as God already sees them means that we would finally see everyone the same. They wouldn't appear different to us in any way. They would be a direct reflection of God, perfectly made in His own image. We wouldn't see the color of their skin, eyes, or hair color. We wouldn't

The Greatest Gift Ever

notice if they were fat or skinny. We wouldn't notice if they were tall or short. We wouldn't see that there was anything wrong with them at all. We wouldn't notice if they were some how different from us.

Imagine not having the time to be angry or disappointed with someone because you were too busy always, unconditionally giving love to them, no matter what. You wouldn't see anyone's flaws. You would give love to them just as God already always, unconditionally loves you. Everyone would appear as white as snow and, for once, you might also be seen as sinless, just as Jesus Christ was.

Thankfully, we would lose all of those negative emotions and feelings we've learned to harbor towards one another. A "Godly world" with no more hate, no more anger, no more war, no more bias, no more judging, no more fear, no more envy, no more doubt, and no more things that divide us from each other today. A world filled with all of God's love, peace, happiness, and joy. A world like that would also be absent Satan, because he wouldn't exist in a perfect world. In a perfect world, no one would fall for any of his lies.

There wouldn't be any reason for you not to always, unconditionally give love to others, no matter what, because you would only see others as God already sees them. Just as God has and always will see you, you, too, would see everyone else as perfect reflections of God.

The only way you're going to make that kind of a world a reality is if you choose to begin to transform your heart, your mind, and your soul. You have to change everything you do and everything you say, unless you're already approaching it with Godly love. You have to stop seeing the world through your eyes and begin to see the world through God's eyes. Only then will you ever see a positive change in the world, one Christian at a time, through one random act of Godly love at a time.

So there you have it. A truly "from God"-inspired book from an ordinary Joe who finally learned what was the greatest gift ever and how that new discovery changed my life forever. I shared my struggles so you, too, could see that change can take many years and that you'll inevitably face certain obstacles along your journey. But if you stand fast in your faith, surrender all, and totally trust God you, too, can change in ways you never thought possible before. If I can begin to change, then I know you can change as well.

The Greatest Gift Ever

Make that life-altering decision to begin your journey today, right here, right now. No more excuses. No more ifs, ands, or buts. No more stipulations, conditions, prenuptials, or any date-time stamps. Don't let another day go by without beginning your transformation. You can't afford to take for granted that there will always be a tomorrow. You can't take for granted that you'll always have the time to make things right.

Start the change within you right now. Pray to God for the strength, courage, and commitment to always, unconditionally give love to others, no matter what. This process won't be easy, but stay the course. You'll experience good days and bad days, but the more you transform, the calmer the seas will become around you. Keep your eyes on the prize.

All the things that exist outside of God will be challenging and will resist all your efforts to transform. You'll encounter others who will try to convince you it isn't worth it. You'll experience resistance from your loved ones, family, friends, and even strangers. Satan will constantly attack you and try to gain a foothold in your life to keep you from completing your transformation. Once you start don't quit.

New Beginnings

1 Corinthians 10:13 – "No temptation has overtaken you but such as is common to man; and God is faithful, who will not allow you to be tempted beyond what you are able, but with the temptation will provide the way of escape also, so that you'll be able to endure it." (NASB)

James 1:15-17 – "When a person is carried away with desire, lured by lust, and when desire becomes the focus and takes control, it gives birth to sin. *When* sin becomes fully grown, it produces death.

If you give in to temptation and desire, then sin is born. If you give in to sin long enough, it overpowers you and costs you your life.

My dearly loved brothers and sisters, don't be misled. Every good gift bestowed, every perfect gift received comes *to us* from above, courtesy of the Father of lights. He *is consistent.* He won't change His mind or play tricks in the shadows." (VOICE)

Don't lose hope and no matter what, don't ever give up. It will all be worth it in the end. One minute at a time, one hour at a time, and one day at a time.

Keep your eyes focused on the prize and know that you, too, can do it. With God on your side, who can be against you?

Psalm 139:13-14, 16 – "You made all the delicate, inner parts of my body and knit me together in my mother's womb. Thank you for making me so wonderfully complex! Your workmanship is marvelous—how well I know it. You saw me before I was born. Every day of my life was recorded in your book. Every moment was laid out before a single day had passed." (NLT)

2 Corinthians 13:11 – "Finally, brothers and sisters, rejoice! Strive for full restoration, encourage one another, be of one mind, live in peace. And the God of love and peace will be with you." (NIV)

I CHOOSE LOVE
(MY PRAYER FOR YOU, THE READER)

Heavenly Father – I am eternally grateful to You for allowing me to become Your child. I know I don't deserve my salvation. You gave it to me, even though at my very core I'm nothing more than a sinner. I entered into Your family when I chose to believe that You so loved me that You gave Your one and only Son as the ultimate sacrifice so that I may have eternal life.

Help me to always believe that my salvation came with no strings attached. Allow me to release any bondage I may be harboring inside that falsely makes me feel I have to some how earn Your love or that I have to keep proving myself to You. Allow me to bury any baggage I've carried over the years that allowed Satan to gain a foothold in my life that

The Greatest Gift Ever

keeps me from always, unconditionally giving my love to You.

Help me to finally, fully surrender all of me to You. Thank you for revealing Your perfect love blueprint to me. Let that same Godly love transform me so that I, too, can mature in my Christian journey and become more like Your son Jesus Christ each and every day.

Right here, right now, help me to always choose to always, unconditionally give my love to all, no matter what. Let others see You in me by allowing Your love to always flow outwardly from inside of me for the rest of my life. In all that I say and all that I do, let Your love guide, overpower, and consume me. Allow me to finally see Your world and all its beauty through Your eyes. Help me to make Your world even more beautiful by doing my part every day. Thank you for always, unconditionally giving Your love to me, no matter what.

In Jesus Christ's name I pray–Amen.

MY GOD

Lord, I want to know You like You know me;
To hear Your heartbeat as You do mine;
To know Your voice and to feel Your soul;
To one day to be as close to You as You have always been to me,
From now until the end of my time.

Lord, I am nothing more than a sinner,
But because of the love of Christ I am a winner,
Bonded to You and Heaven forever.
Thankfully there will never be anything better.

Help the ears of my heart to hear
Your sweet spoken voice's message that is always crystal clear;
To freely give Godly love to all,

The Greatest Gift Ever

Because that will remain Your heavenly call.
Lord, please tear down every wall
That keeps me from always giving love to
All that exists in Your perfect world,
Every person and everything You created.
Teach me what it means to finally be
Liberated and set free,
Maturing into that Christian You formed inside me.

I'm longing for the life You envisioned for me,
Strip away all my pride.
I'm ready to walk with You in stride,
Always being by Your side.
I'm tired of all the pain I hold deep down inside.
Mold me, shape me, free me,
Make me into an amazing reflection of You
So everyone can forever see You within me.

Change my heart Lord,
Change my soul,
Change my mind,
Oh, I've got so far to go
To finally become the person
You made me to be.

My God

I want to know You like You know me;
To be as close to You as You are to me;
To hear Your heartbeat as You do mine;
To know Your soul as You know mine.

Teach me how to love You
The way You have always loved me,
With all my heart and soul,
With all my mind,
From now till the end of time.

I want to know the love
That only comes from You;
A love that remains steadfast and true,
Guiding me my whole life through.

I know I'll never stop sinning,
But I'll leave this earth winning;
Instead of taking the easy road like the rest,
Forever living in harmony with You,
Striving one day to become one of the best of
the best.

Amen

__MY FINAL DAY__

Through God's love and grace,
You humbly took Your place,
Carrying that cross of wood
To the mount where it stood;
For the whole world would eventually get to see
The ultimate sacrifice You were called to be.

You endured such ridicule and torture,
No one could ever imagine the horror.
There were so many who didn't believe
The greatness You were bound to achieve.
Until Your final breath
You stayed true to Your quest.

For God so loved the world
He freely gave His one and only son

My Final Day

So that even a sinner like me
Will one day shout out with glee.
When my time here on earth is done,
My eternal life with You will have just begun.

Truth be told,
I can't wait to behold
The holiness and majesty of Your face,
As I enter into Your amazing holy space,
Knowing all my sins have been forgiven
As You welcome me to Heaven.

Until my final day,
I will strive to walk in all Your ways.
Holding onto the truth
I have believed since my youth,
Finally getting to see all of God's beauty and grace
As I ascend into Your glorious heavenly place.

Father, please help me to always keep my heart
fixed on You – Amen.

BIBLIOGRAPHY

Stetzer, E. (2009, March 9). Barna: How Many Have a Biblical Worldview? Retrieved Fall 2015, from Christianitytoday.com

BibleGateway (n.d.). Retrieved Spring 2016, from https://www.biblegateway.com/

Agape. (2016, May 24). In *Wikipedia, The Free Encyclopedia*. Retrieved 18:56, May 25, 2016, from https://en.wikipedia.org/w/index.php?title=Agape&oldid=721930700

Dictionary, Encyclopedia and Thesaurus. (n.d.). Retrieved Spring 2016, from http://www.thefreedictionary.com

Love, Definition of Love by Merriam-Webster. 2005. 25 May. 2016, from http://www.merriam-webster.com /dictionary/love

32 Shocking Divorce Statistics. (2012, October 12). Retrieved Fall 2015 http://www.mckinley-irvin.com/Family-Law-Blog/2012/October/32-Shocking-Divorce-Statistics.aspx

Groeschel, C., & Groeschel, A. (2014). From this day forward: Five commitments to fail-proof your marriage. Grand Rapids, MI: Zondervan.

Anderson, N. T. (2000). Victory over the darkness: Realizing the power of your identity in Christ. Ventura, CA: Regal Books.

Foster, R. J. (1989). Celebration of discipline. Hodder & Stoughton.

West, Matthew. "Forgiveness." By Matthew West. Into the Light. Sparrow Records, 2012. CD.

Dixon, Colton. "Let Them See You." By Colton Dixon. A Messenger. Sparrow Records, 2013. CD.

Mike + The Mechanics. "The Living Years." By Rutherford and B. A. Robertson. Living Years. Atlantic Records, 1988. CD.

Wilson, Josh. "That Was Then, This Is Now." By Josh Wilson. That Was Then, This Is Now. Sparrow Records, 2015. CD.

CPSIA information can be obtained
at www.ICGtesting.com
Printed in the USA
BVOW11s2105271216
471979BV00001B/1/P

9 781498 483032